MW00426514

Discover Your DIVINITY

A MODERN GUIDE
TO AFFIRMATIVE PRAYER

LINDA MARTELLA-WHITSETT
AND DEEANN WEIR MORENCY

Discover Your
DIVINITY
A MODERN GUIDE
TO AFFIRMATIVE PRAYER

unity®
Books

Unity Village, MO 64065-0001

DISCOVER YOUR DIVINITY

©2023 by Linda Martella-Whitsett and DeeAnn Weir Morency. All rights reserved. No part of this book may be used or reproduced in any manner whatsoever without written permission from Unity School of Christianity, dba Unity World Headquarters, except in the case of brief quotations included in critical articles and reviews or in the newsletters and lesson plans of licensed Unity teachers or ministers. For information, address Unity Books, Publishers, 1901 NW Blue Parkway, Unity Village, MO 64065-0001. To place an order, call the Customer Care Department at 816-969-2069 or visit us at *unity.org*.

Bible quotations from the American Standard Version unless otherwise noted.

First edition 2023

Cover and interior design: Hailee Pavey

ISBN: 978-0-87159-426-6
eISBN: 978-0-87159-912-4
Library of Congress
Catalog Card Number: 2023931108
Canada GST: R132529033

DEDICATIONS

From Linda:

To countless courageous colleagues, students, friends, and family discovering their divinity and shining light in the world.

From DeeAnn:

To my wife, Christina.
To all those drawn to a life of prayer and who are willing to joyfully illuminate the I AM we all are.

TABLE OF CONTENTS

INTRODUCTION

The writing of this book has been a journey. It is the culmi-nation of more than four years of collaboration dedicated to exploring, clarifying, and ultimately reconceptualizing the Unity affirmative prayer process. Affirmative prayer transformed both of our lives, and we will be sharing with you the insights of our lifelong exploration of the affirmative prayer process.

Our journey began with our personal, transformational experiences of prayer long before we actually knew each other. For DeeAnn that meant a ray of hope in the midst of deepest despair; for Linda it was moving past disillusionment into true empowerment.

DeeAnn

My story is one that so many of us have lived. My heart was breaking. After 13 years I suddenly found myself facing a very painful, ugly divorce, and my world was in turmoil. The busi-ness we had built together was gone, the community of friends and colleagues we had created scattered, and all my dreams for a life together broken.

From the depths of pain I sought out New Thought spiritual communities for support. While the messages were uplifting, they were not enough to shift my despair and hopelessness. Every Sunday there was an open invitation to pray with a prayer practitioner after service. Driven by desperation, one Sunday morning I finally stepped outside my comfort zone and asked for prayer. In that moment, my life was forever changed.

As I poured out my story of loss, pain, disillusionment, anger, and betrayal, the prayer practitioner, whom I had never met before, listened with compassion and then invited me to join her in an affirmative prayer. What happened next was revolutionary. She did not join me in my story of brokenness, she did not pray to a God outside of me to take away my pain. Instead, she met every aspect of my story with what she knew to be the truth of me, my divine identity.

She spoke of love and healing, of my innate capacity to be love and to be loved. She spoke of possibility and divine potential. She saw through the broken, desperate woman I felt myself to be and affirmed the strong, capable, empowered, and loving woman I actually was. She held up a divine mirror for me to see myself anew. She spoke with such surety and declared who I truly was with such clarity that I was able to catch a glimpse of myself as she saw me. In that moment I remembered something about myself, something essential was reawakened, and for the first time in forever I felt hope.

That moment changed me and sparked a healing journey that has brought me more joy, love, and happiness than I ever thought possible. Something within me shifted and as it shifted, the story I was telling shifted as well. Pain was no longer all I could see or feel. In that moment I remembered who I truly was. I have never forgotten the relief and freedom of that remembering. I say with all honestly, affirmative prayer saved my life.

Linda

At the age of 19, a shooting star landed at the base of my spine and traveled up and out the crown of my head. I was driving at the time. Moving the car over to the side of the highway and parking, I entered a state of blissful awareness of oneness. Fleeting though it was, my experience launched an adult life dedicated to the invisible but sensed reality that is spirituality.

Within a year, I would be initiated into a yoga practice that activated Shakti, spiritual vitality, leading to multiple, frequent moments of oneness. I sensed the truth in my teacher's refrain: "The guru is within."

I found myself far from the religious tradition of my childhood. God no longer seemed an external, separate being. I no longer seemed a solid, separate being. Everything changed. I changed, able to resolve inner discords by attuning to inexhaustible, infinite power that I could experience and express.

Years later when raising my children, I wanted a community for them in which they could experience oneness. Attending my first Unity Sunday service, I heard, "There is only one power and one presence in the universe and in my life." I wept in recognition. God is within.

Fast-forwarding through a few decades of study and credentialing in Unity leadership, I found I was struggling with prayer. Much of what I had been reading and hearing smacked of separation, calling out to Father-Mother God or Sweet Precious Spirit. My own prayers, following the models of my teachers, became ineffectual. I hungered for the sense of oneness I had known very well but that now seemed elusive.

I resumed study, no longer toward a credentialing goal but expressly for me, to revive my prayer life in honesty and truth. With fervor, I dove into classic Unity literature on prayer. I was stunned to find key teachings that had not been emphasized in my training but resonated with my experience.

Myrtle Fillmore's writings confirmed my inclination toward the Truth of oneness:

> Prayers aren't sent out at all! Sometimes that is
> our trouble. Where would we send our prayers?

We should direct them to our minds and hearts and affairs.—*Myrtle Fillmore's Healing Letters*

Charles Fillmore defined prayer as:

More than supplication ... an affirmation of Truth that eternally exists; the act of affirmation ... the "yes" action of the mind; the act of affirming; the declaring of Truth; the mental movement that asserts confidently and persistently the Truth of Being in the face of all appearances to the contrary.—*The Revealing Word*

And Eric Butterworth taught:

The true affirmation is: *I AM*. This was the key to Jesus' power—his affirmation and realization of I AM. Not "I want to be," "I hope to be," "I will be someday," or "Dear Lord, make me to be." But simply: *I AM*.—Eric Butterworth, *The Universe Is Calling*

Diving into practice with renewed purpose, I found that by acknowledging the truth of one power and describing one power in an actionable way—as life, as love, as wisdom, as strength—I transformed my experience time and again. I healed many years of separation from my father by claiming I AM love. I healed the terror I had felt about my son's service in the Gulf War by claiming I AM faith, imagination, and unity (love). I healed a consciousness of lack when I worried about money and work by claiming I AM wisdom, order, and will. Prayer led to empowerment.

Why This Book Now?

This is about the power of affirmative prayer. It is about the power of praying by ourselves and praying with others from an awareness of our spiritual nature and is meant to facilitate deep healing and support personal empowerment. Affirmative prayer is about seeing and naming the truth that already is, even if it is difficult to recognize. It is this unique aspect of affirmative prayer that makes it so worthwhile to explore, even if you already have a powerful prayer life.

While this book is meant for anyone interested in prayer and praying with others, the approach and underlying principles are distinctly Unity. This book is first and foremost for our Unity community, that we may clarify and strengthen our collective understanding of affirmative prayer.

Years of teaching affirmative prayer has convinced us that confusion about prayer exists within Unity communities. The Unity movement was founded on prayer, the power of agreement, and affirming Truth. Yet within Unity a variety of prayer methods are used, some grounded in Unity teachings, others derivatives of other New Thought communities, and some derivatives from other faith traditions and denominations. In our travels we have heard prayers at Unity communities that resonate with the more traditional Christian faiths, Buddhist and Native-American traditions. There is nothing wrong with praying in whatever way we may pray; however, Unity has a rich and powerful history with a very specific and impactful form of prayer—affirmative prayer.

This book offers a cohesive process arising from the historical legacy of Unity that is accessible and dynamic for a modern-day seeker. Our reconceptualized model provides updated language that reflects continually evolving understanding of spiritual principle and affirmative prayer.

Unity is not alone in the evolution of its teachings. Faith traditions around the world continue to evolve, and many have incorporated the powerful teachings of Unity. Affirmations are now commonplace. The idea that we are divine and creators of our experience is now shared by a wide range of Christian denominations and other faiths. Yet affirmative prayer is still something unique to New Thought. Unity has long been the most visible carrier of this spiritual practice through our far-reaching, 24-hour prayer ministry, Silent Unity®. Affirmative prayer is ours to offer to the world, and what a gift it is!

How to Use This Book

This book is designed for everyone who wishes to deepen their personal prayer life and who feels called to pray with others. It is for laypeople, prayer associates, prayer circles, spiritual practitioners, and ministers of Unity, Centers for Spiritual Living, or Divine Science as well as any other denomination. This book seeks to provide guidance and clarity as to how the affirmative prayer process we have been teaching supports both the one praying and the one receiving prayer. We will examine foundational principles to cultivate your own personal prayer life as well as how to flow through prayer when praying with others.

Chapter 1 gives the reader an overview and understanding of this unique prayer form. The remaining chapters in this first section look at the foundational spiritual principles of affirmative prayer and how we can harness and activate our divine creative potential. Chapter 4 examines the consciousness of affirming and how to master these essential building blocks.

In the next section, we look at our own personal prayer life and how we embody, understand, and live these spiritual principles. Chapters 5 and 6 invite a deep exploration into our understanding of God, our innate divinity, and how to activate our spiritual capacities. Chapter 7 provides an in-depth look at the five movements of prayer and how this flow can powerfully transform consciousness. We conclude this section with Chapter 8, titled "When Prayer Seems Not to be Working," containing guidance about spiritual realization.

The last section is dedicated to how we pray with others. Chapters 9 and 10 offer guidance as you shift from your personal prayer life to the joy of praying with others, and includes best practices, how to navigate some common challenges, and considerations for developing style and vocabulary when praying with others. Chapter 11 provides instructions for the flow of prayer when our focus is on praying with others. The final chapter offers concrete processes to continue evolving your prayer practice and prayer consciousness.

Affirmative prayer is a powerful tool for awakening, embodying, and activating our most authentic self. Whether you are an experienced prayer practitioner or new to the wonders of affirmative prayer, there is always more to discover about ourselves, our divine nature, and how we can live into truth more fully. This particular process has been honed and fine-tuned with prayer chaplains in a variety of Unity communities. The impact has been profound, both for the prayer chaplains and for the communities they serve. As with any new process, there has also been some resistance. Resistance is a wonderful opportunity for growth and transformation! We invite you to immerse yourself in the process and explore what else is possible in your own prayer life and in the prayer life of your community. Experiment and explore—and who knows what you might discover about yourself and the world in the process?

Our intention and blessing are that your engagement with this book will be valuable, and that you will be more certain of your divine identity than ever before. We bless you with a bold and authentic claim on the mandate Charles Fillmore proclaimed in *Talks on Truth*: "You can attain to everything you can imagine. If you can imagine that it is possible to God, it is also possible to you."

CHAPTER 1

WHAT IS AFFIRMATIVE PRAYER?

Traditionally, and almost universally, prayer is understood as a solemn request or a statement of thanks addressed to a deity or higher power. It presumes human powerlessness and divine intervention toward a desired outcome.

Affirmative prayer is a completely different form of prayer. The teaching of *oneness*—meaning there is only one divine power and therefore God and humanity are one in absolute Truth—changes prayer. Rather than presuming the power we seek is outside and separate from us, affirmative prayer empowers us to respond to life's circumstances by drawing upon the Truth of oneness. We can recognize, claim, and embody the fullness of our divinity in the midst of our human experience.

The Truth we affirm is the reality of God as the one and only power behind all that can be. The Truth is the one and only power within us and all around us, our divine identity. The Truth is that we are ever able to recognize and realize our divine nature by which we can express abundant life, love, strength, and faith amidst any circumstance.

What we achieve through means of affirmative prayer is not a specific outcome, but a spiritual authority to claim and realize our own spiritual power. Affirmative prayer doesn't change the Divine. Affirmative prayer changes us.

Definition of Affirmative Prayer

Prayer as taught in this book is affirmative rather than supplicatory. Defining affirmative prayer, Unity cofounder Charles Fillmore taught:

> Prayer is more than supplication. It is an affirmation of Truth that eternally exists, but which has not yet come into consciousness. It comes into consciousness not by supplication but by affirmation.
>
> —*The Revealing Word*

An affirmation is a statement of Truth used as an anchor for our mind. Just as we know the sun is always shining behind a cloudy sky, we can know the truth about wholeness, abundance, and harmony while moving through illness, financial strain, and disharmony.

Recognize that wholeness, abundance, and harmony are examples of ways we can describe the power of God. That power, we realize in prayer, is the power within us as well as around us. In prayer, we begin to see that we are not therefore powerless; in fact, we are powerfully able to cooperate with the ideal of wholeness, abundance, and harmony.

Affirmative prayer is empowering prayer. The founder of the Religious Science movement, Ernest Holmes, said:

> The limitless resources of the Spirit are at our command. The power of the infinite is at our disposal.
>
> —Ernest Holmes, *Richer Living*

Other definitions for affirmative prayer include transformational mind action and spiritual realization.

Transformational Mind Action

Affirmative prayer is based in the creative power of mind. Our thoughts and beliefs are creative, meaning that our outlook, attitudes, expectations, and worldview are reinforced in our experiences. We tend to see what we expect to see and to interpret the world around us according to our developed beliefs. When we don't like what we see, the good news is that we can change our thoughts and beliefs.

Affirmative prayer is recognized as "the most highly accelerated mind action known. It steps up mental action until [one's] consciousness synchronizes with the Christ mind" (Fillmore, *The Revealing Word*).

Ernest Holmes taught that prayer treatment "is the time, process, and method necessary to the changing of our thought" (Holmes, *Science of Mind*).

Our work is to shift from human, or relative, thinking to spiritual, or absolute thinking. We pray because we feel powerless in some circumstances and we seek a remedy, solution, or improvement. Affirmative prayer is a quest for and fulfillment of spiritual power. To be effective in affirmative prayer is to elevate human thinking to the level of oneness, where we have access to absolute Truth.

Spiritual Realization

Affirmative prayer offers an empowering framework for transformation. It is not attempting to get anything from God or even speaking *to* God. Affirmative prayer is rooted in the radical idea that each of us is a spiritual or divine human. It invites us to speak *from* our divine nature and to tell the Truth to our human circumstances.

True prayer is not asking for things, not even the best of things. Prayer is the lifting of the consciousness to the place where these things are.

—Sue Sikking, *A Letter to Adam*

When we declare and celebrate our divine nature, we live life with more abundance, freedom, joy, and love. Affirmative prayer enables us to remember our spiritual self and live from an inner awareness of possibility and potential. It provides a pathway for clearing away limiting beliefs and false ideas about who we think we are. It allows us to boldly declare the spiritual truth that we are and to realize just how much more is possible in our life.

Affirmative prayer reminds us, and anyone with whom we are praying, that there is a deeper Truth for us to realize, underneath and aside from the present circumstance. Anyone can learn, practice, and master the process of shifting awareness away from a situation or condition to the deeper spiritual Truth that is always operating and always available for us to claim.

An access point to spiritual realization, affirmative prayer is the practice of recognizing oneness, integrating our human and divine identity, and realizing we are fully able to respond to life's circumstances by means of innate spiritual power. With spiritual authority, we realize or understand our capacity to change the way we have been thinking and behaving. Affirmative prayer changes us. When we change, our experience changes and we can change our circumstances.

Distinguishing Features of Affirmative Prayer

As you proceed in the study of affirmative prayer, it may be helpful to keep in mind these distinguishing features:

Affirming Rather Than Supplicating

Shifting from supplicating to affirming, we let go of the thought of the Divine as a separate being with human-like per-

13

sonality. In Chapters 2 and 5 you will find further explanation and instruction about the nature of the Divine. Meanwhile, think about the usefulness of letting go of the thought of God as a deity to beseech or to bargain with during times of human need. Affirming is about recognizing a universal, reliable spiritual Truth and claiming our spiritual power. Affirming is essentially activating spiritual power.

Referring to the Divine in Terms of Powers and Principles

Shifting from God as a deity who acts to God as power or principle itself, we relieve ourselves of the problem of a God assumed to have human characteristics and motives. While it may seem awkward at first to eliminate anthropomorphic descriptors for the Divine, our ability to claim and realize divine identity depends upon broadening an understanding of the nature of the Divine. For a more thorough explanation of how to define the Divine in ways that we can claim, read Chapters 5 and 6.

Highlighting Oneness

Shifting from duality to oneness, we subscribe to the knowledge of only one power, divine power, and we recognize that all the power that ever is, is right here and right now. We are able to integrate the nature of the Divine with human nature, to become convinced we are divine humans with spiritual authority. To realize we are divine humans is frequently a stumbling block for metaphysicians. We are able to relate to oneness as a concept but not as a reality. It's hard to give up the idea that there is God and there is me. It's hard to claim oneness with an external God or an undefinable God. Identifying recognizable attributes of God allows us to see those attributes in ourselves, so that we can claim and embody them. Affirmative prayer helps us activate spiritual principles, divine qualities, and our divine nature. Chapters 6 and 7 have more to say.

Empowering

Shifting from powerlessness to empowerment, we become responsible for aligning our further thoughts and actions with the power or principle we claim. Myrtle Fillmore taught:

> Our spiritual ministry is only half done unless we give those unto whom we minister an explanation of the Christ principles that will enable them to demonstrate spiritual laws for themselves.

We want to leave a period of prayer with more than a feeling of having been comforted. We want the confidence to think, speak, and act differently than before, empowered to improve the situation. We have hold of a spiritual tool now, a way of practicing that makes a difference; that our spiritual shift leads to a shift in our behavior that positively affects the situation. Not magical thinking that God will act; instead, our inspired and enlightened actions change our experience.

Affirmative prayer is unique in this respect. Its power lies in how it is *not* like other forms of prayer. Other forms of prayer may include supplication, bargaining with God, asking for help from an intervener such as a saint or bodhisattva, or surrendering to an external force. There are some clear differences that distinguish affirmative prayer from other forms of prayer.

What Affirmative Prayer Is Not:

- Manipulating or coercing people or events to bring about some personally desired change.

- Attempting to "reach" God. God is already here, always present and accessible.

- Persuading God to "change his mind" or suspend universal laws on our behalf.

- Putting our own willpower into changing a condition; trying to overcome God's seeming "reluctance" to "right" an apparent wrong.

- Surrendering in the conventional meaning of the word, giving up and handing the situation over to an external force.

- Denying that a person is experiencing sickness. Illness and suffering do exist in human experience.

- Disallowing other forms of healing, such as medicine, surgery, psychiatry, diet, and so on.

- Attempting to exert spiritual control of the material universe, as though they were separate entities.

- Thinking that the one praying is doing the healing.

What Affirmative Prayer Is:

- Consciously clearing away false beliefs to reveal the Truth that is always there.

- Allowing ourselves to realize and declare the spiritual truth about ourselves and the condition we are praying about.

- Being still and knowing that God Is, and letting that reality be felt so clearly that we can realize and declare the spiritual truth of any situation.

- Surrendering in the sense of releasing our human-centric perspective and yielding to our divine identity.

- Accepting that every new discovery in medical fields is a revelation of Truth arising from universal wisdom.

- Understanding that mind in essence and mind in form are one and the same, so there is no difference between our thoughts and beliefs and what they become.

- Realizing that since a human being is a divine human, there is a perfect spiritual idea that is the Truth of every individual, no matter what they are experiencing, and this Truth can be realized and declared.

Affirmative prayer is anchored in our divine humanity. It asks us to move past petitioning, begging, pleading, or trying to get God to do something for us. It is about our own awakening to what we are capable of being and doing in the world when we remember our spiritual identity.

Affirmations

At the heart of affirmative prayer lies the transformational power of affirmations. The popularity and widespread use of affirmations speak to their effectiveness. Affirmations declare the truth of who we are. Affirmative prayer builds upon, amplifies, and increases that power exponentially.

Here are some examples of affirmations:

I am love in action.

I am open and willing to do all that is mine to do.

I am strong and capable.

I am empowered and I joyfully empower others.

I am the power of plenty, gratefully giving and receiving.

I am faith-filled and faithful.

These simple, declarative statements of Truth have the power to override our insecurities, fears, and doubts. They help us see past a circumstance to the spiritual truth. Affirmations are not hopes or wishes. Affirmations are not magic. Affirmations are tools for remembering an absolute Truth about ourselves—to own something we perhaps have never realized was true. Affirmations remind us of and realign us with our true nature, and it is our true nature that has the power to transform our false beliefs.

We will further explore the power of affirmations in Chapter 4.

The two of us, DeeAnn and Linda, have devoted years to exploring, clarifying, and teaching affirmative prayer. The prayer process outlined in this book arose from the desire to make affirmative prayer accessible and understandable to a contemporary audience. To that end we have designed a "prayer flow," rooted in New Thought spiritual principle and previous affirmative prayer models, that facilitates the recognition and realization of true spiritual power.

The affirmative prayer process, explained in the chapters to come, involves a series of movements, a flow from recognizing the nature of God as a power or principle, integrating the concept that I AM that power or principle in Truth, and therefore realizing I can do or say or think or act in alignment with the power or principle. The flow of affirmative prayer ultimately transforms and empowers us. It is not really a step-by-step, paint-by-numbers formula. It is more akin to the opening of a frond on a fern. Affirmative prayer is a progression of movements that flow toward a new awareness. We can also imagine this prayer flow as a spiral opening within us, opening toward a new understanding.

The five movements that make up the affirmative prayer flow:

I **open** to new possibility.

I **recognize** God Is.

I **integrate** I AM.

I **realize** I can, I have, I know.

I **appreciate** the shift in consciousness.

Each movement leads to the next. As we inhabit each movement, our consciousness, like a fern frond, unfurls from the tension of a prayer concern toward the expansiveness of divine realization. It is in the realization movement that we can concretely activate the divinity that we are.

You will be reading much more about each of these movements, but here is an initial overview:

I open: The first moments of affirmative prayer establish our readiness, openness, and willingness for a new possibility, a divine understanding. Our willingness to open to something new is what creates the space for a shift in consciousness.

I recognize God Is: From this place of open willingness, we then recognize and name what God is. Recognizing a specific divine principle or power is key to the movement in prayer toward spiritual realization.

I integrate I AM: Once we recognize God Is a specific principle or power, we then integrate that divine principle and understand it as our being-ness.

I realize I can, I have, I know: From this integrated awareness of our oneness, we can now realize the spiritual truth of any situation. We can realize what we can do, what we know, what we have available to us. It is in realization that we activate a divine principle in time and space.

I appreciate the shift in consciousness: The final movement of the prayer is actually appreciation for our shift in consciousness, appreciation for the new understanding, and appreciation that the prayer itself brought about a realization of Truth.

We will be exploring the foundational principles and purpose for each movement in great depth in subsequent chapters, beginning with the spiritual principles that support the second, third, and fourth movements, which we call the heart of affirmative prayer:

Recognizing God Is: We name a power or principle that would be useful right now.

Integrating I AM: We integrate that power or principle as the truth of being.

Realizing I can, I have, I know: We can now live into this principle in a new way.

By understanding the foundational principles that support affirmative prayer, we can more deeply embody this powerfully transformative practice.

REFLECT AND PRACTICE

◎ What is your current prayer practice and what excites you or entices you to learn more about affirmative prayer?

◎ What does it mean to you to feel empowered in your prayer life?

◎ What comes up for you when you read: *What we get by means of affirmative prayer is not a specific outcome [but] spiritual authority to claim and realize spiritual power?*

◎ Reviewing the distinguishing features of affirmative prayer, which do you question? Write about it or share with a study partner.

◎ How do you understand surrender? What arises for you at the idea of yielding into your divine identity rather than an external force?

◎ Selecting one of the chapter's examples of affirmations, what do you imagine you can do knowing this about yourself?

◎ At the start of each day this week, write an affirmation to guide your actions throughout the day.

CHAPTER 2

Oneness, the Prime Principle

Now that we have defined affirmative prayer and seen an overview of the prayer flow, we can explain the principles and teachings that form the foundation for affirmative prayer. These principles provide a framework that supports an awakened understanding of our true nature.

We begin with focus on oneness, the key or prime principle at the heart of spiritual understanding.

What Is Principle?

A principle is a fact or a Truth that is constant and has no opposite. An example of a simple mathematical principle we learn early on is 2+2=4. No matter where you are, or what you are doing, or how you are doing it, 2+2 will always equal 4. If you arrive at 3 or 5, the error is yours. The principle is neutral, neither good nor bad, which means it can be used constructively or destructively. When used constructively, the invisible principle leads to positive, visible effects in our lived experience. When used destructively, the visible effects show up as negative experience. This principle is active in our lives whether we consciously use it or not.

What is also true about principles is that they build on each other. Mastering addition allows us to master multiplication. Mastering subtraction allows us to master division. Mastering multiplication and division allows us to master fractions and so on and so forth. Each principle leads to another. The stronger our foundational understanding of mathematics, the easier it is for us to move into the more complicated areas of algebra and calculus.

Many principles or laws are active in our world. They have always been active—whether or not we have been aware of them. The law of gravity is a principle that Isaac Newton did not create—he identified it. Once this law was identified it could then be studied and more deeply understood. We don't question gravity. We don't fight with gravity. Gravity is. It is operating in our lives, and we use it to the best of our ability. We may lift weights to build our muscles, which is one way to use the law of gravity. We may invert ourselves to stretch our backs. Anytime we are using levers and counterweights to move, lift, and build, we are consciously using the law of gravity in ways that work for us. And because principles can be combined, we may choose to exercise in a swimming pool and use the principle of buoyancy to consciously mitigate the effect and impact of the law of gravity.

Spiritual principle works the same way. While we cannot see the law of buoyancy or the law of gravity, we can feel the effects of these laws on our lives. Behind all that is visible lies the invisible. We don't have to see it or agree with it for it to impact our lives. Spiritual principle is active right now whether we understand it, whether we agree with it, and whether we acknowledge it. It is always active.

We evolve and grow spiritually by developing mastery in the use of spiritual principle to support our lived experience. Affirmative prayer is a powerful spiritual technology that supports mastery, transformation, and healing of personal, limited beliefs. When we pray with others, affirmative prayer supports others in their journey toward spiritual liberation.

Oneness, the Prime Principle

Oneness is the foundational spiritual principle that affirmative prayer is built upon. Oneness is a changeless Truth, a constant within consciousness. As the prime principle, it is the constant from which every other physical and spiritual principle arises. Oneness is found in the mystical teachings of many faith traditions. By its very nature, oneness includes the God of all faith traditions as well as any recognized spiritual power.

Oneness means there is one and only one true power in all of life, whether you name it divine mind, Spirit, God, consciousness, or the Universe. Oneness by its very nature is indivisible; there is nothing that can be separate or outside of it. Oneness cannot be split or dual. It is whole, always. And if nothing is outside of oneness, you cannot be separate from oneness. All are one, even as the One may be experienced and understood in infinite ways.

> God is the name we give to that unchangeable, inexorable principle at the source of all existence.
> —H. Emilie Cady, *Lessons in Truth*

The principle of oneness, this singular power, is not a person but the very essence of life, the organizing principle and formless intelligence out of which everything and everyone comes into existence. All physical and spiritual principles are contained within oneness.

> Principle does not occupy space; neither has it any limitations of time or matter, but it eternally exists as the one underlying cause out of which come forth all true ideas.
> —Charles Fillmore, *The Revealing Word*

With oneness as the prime principle, just as addition leads to subtraction, we can begin to identify other Truth principles that naturally arise from oneness. In Unity there are three very clear defining principles and characteristics of oneness called the three omnis: omnipresence, omniscience, and omnipotence. Just as you are not separate from the principle of oneness, you also are not separate from the principles of omnipresence, omniscience, and omnipotence.

You may be familiar with some version of the three omnis from religious studies. *Omni* as a prefix relates to all there is, everywhere, and everything. Note these three characteristics are not adjectives, they are nouns. The principles of omnipresence, omniscience, and omnipotence do not describe a personal, human-like quality that is unique to a deity. They are constants themselves, always present, always active, and always available to you.

Omnipresence is pervasiveness, indicating spiritual power is not centralized in a single location but is everywhere. A popular prayer in Unity concludes with "Wherever I am, God is!" as a reminder that all that God is—all divine ideas—are present everywhere. Linda's word for omnipresence is *everywhereness*, acknowledging we are not limited by human form. In fact *presence* can be experienced nonlocally. We prove this principle when we log on to Zoom with people from around the world, or when we speak with someone over the telephone, or when we commune with a deceased loved one.

Omniscience means the capacity of knowingness. All knowledge is available and we have the innate ability to know. We prove this principle when we think of a friend then they call us or send a text; when we know what our next step is, even if it doesn't seem to make logical sense; or when we meet someone and we know that person, even if we have never actually met them before.

Omnipotence means the capacity of powerfulness. All power is available and we have the innate ability to be powerful. This capacity is limitless. We always have the capacity to be powerful. We demonstrate omnipotence when we finally stand up and speak our truth, when we find the strength to accomplish what seemed impossible, or when we quiet our fears and manage to keep moving forward.

These three principles are active in our life right now. In affirmative prayer, we consciously use and activate these spiritual principles. This is important to remember: Principle does not use us; we use principle.

Goodness

In the way that subtraction leads to division, the three omnis lead us to recognize the nature of oneness in other truth principles. If God is omnipresence, omniscience, and omnipotence, then we can see that goodness also naturally arises. What we mean by goodness is that there is no opposing power. No other. No devil. No adversary. No antichrist. No evil incarnate. Nothing and no one against us.

Classic New Thought often equates God with Good, as in the refrain: one power and one presence, God the Good, omnipotent. To say that God is all good and everywhere present can seem confusing. Notice that this common refrain uses the adjective *omnipotent* rather than the noun *omnipotence*. Implied in this refrain is an anthropomorphized God that is some *thing* that exists *somewhere*. But God is not a being—God is *beingness* itself. God doesn't exist somewhere. The prime principle of oneness invites us to deepen and release any false sense of separation, acknowledging the challenge of recognizing the subtle and not-so-subtle ways we make God a being or place God outside us.

There is an additional challenge when using the traditional word *good*. It automatically conjures up the opposite, *bad*. While the intention of the word *good* is to name a principle that actually has no opposite, that is not the typical use of the word. The typical use of the word *good* is steeped in duality. Rather than continually having to define what we actually mean when we say *good*, we offer *goodness* as clearer nomenclature that we can also more easily claim and demonstrate.

God is not a being or person having life, intelligence, love, power. God is that invisible, intangible, but very real something we call life. God is perfect love and infinite power. God is the total of these, the total of all good, whether manifested or unexpressed.

—H. Emilie Cady, *Lessons in Truth*

To say that God, divine mind, or Oneness is goodness does not mean that everything we see or experience in the relative world is good. It means that goodness—and all the qualities and principles that arise from goodness such as order, harmony, peace, and so on—are available and accessible at every moment regardless of the situation. It may not always seem apparent in the relative realm because, as human beings, we do not always activate our divine nature in constructive and productive ways. Our human brains may argue against goodness, especially when witnessing inexplicable malevolence.

It may be helpful to note that the principle of oneness, like mathematics, is values-neutral and that we, whether intentionally or not, choose our thoughts, words, and actions. We are choosing, consciously or unconsciously, whether we use principles for constructive or destructive purposes.

Affirmative prayer provides us with a tool for consciously aligning our thoughts, words, and actions with our divine goodness, our divine identity rather than our human experience. The more we can embrace the principle of oneness, the more able we become to access our inherent spiritual powers and use them constructively.

We must instill into the mind the fundamental proposition that good is without bounds ... We must get this concept, rather than continuing to think there is a power of evil as opposed to the power of Good. We experience good and evil because we perceive a presence of duality rather than unity.

—Ernest Holmes, Science of Mind

Divine Identity

You may have heard that humans are related to God like a drop of water is to the ocean. You are not a drop of water in the ocean. You can pluck a drop of water from the ocean and it can exist separately from the ocean. You cannot pluck a wave out of the ocean. The wave is the action of the ocean. You are the ocean in motion. All that the ocean is, you are.

When defining oneness, we referred to our ability to express omnipresence, omnipotence, and omniscience. These principles and characteristics of oneness are not limited to God/Source/divine mind. How could they be? As we have said, oneness does not leave you out. You cannot be an exception to oneness. All the ways you might describe the nature of the Divine are descriptors of your divine identity. Yes, you are divine! That means goodness is your nature. When you engage in behaviors that do not appear "good," understand this is not God's doing or against God's will but that you have momentarily forgotten your divine identity.

Just as oneness leads to the three omnis, and the three omnis lead to the principle of goodness, goodness leads to so many more divine ideas, principles, and divine qualities available to us. Do you know God as peace? Then you are peace. Do you know God as wisdom? Then you are wisdom. Do you know God as abundance? Then, yes, you are abundance. This is the power of our innate divine identity.

Truly owning and embracing our divine identity is not easy, particularly when we notice human thoughts and feelings we would not classify as Godlike or when we behave in ways contrary to our loftiest values and principles. We may see the Divine in others but fail to accept it in ourselves. Maybe it's challenging to accept our divine identity because of cultural and religious norms suggesting that being human means being weak and unworthy. Maybe you're thinking that being divine would require saintliness or perfection. Or maybe it simply seems too big an assignment! Who among us could wield the full power of God?

We have good news for you. You never have to—in fact you never could—be all that God is in any moment of human experience. You only have to claim and to be one quality of God, just one in any moment. In a moment of need for strength, you can claim divine strength and stand steady in the midst of shifting circumstances. In a moment of need for harmony, you can claim the harmonious power of divine love and think harmonious thoughts. In a moment of need for creativity, you can claim and embody divine imagination. It's easier to claim *I am strength, love, and imagination* than to say *I am God*. It's also easier to think and act according to these capacities.

In New Thought, whose roots lie in the Judeo-Christian faith traditions, our innate divine identity can also be referred to as Christ consciousness. Not to be confused with Jesus the person, Christ consciousness, Buddha consciousness, Atman presence, and the I AM, are all various ways to reference the fullest expression of our divine identity. As we wrestle with our innate worthiness to embody *I am God, I am Buddha, I am Christ*, words from Unity cofounder Charles Fillmore offer great wisdom.

In typewritten notes from 1923, Fillmore wrote that as the offspring of one universal spirit, or God, you can rightfully declare *I am Christ*. The full realization of your Christ identity comes as you demonstrate it:

> And you begin your demonstration wherever you are. You can take it in small bites. You can say, *I am life*, and you will get life; you can say, *I am love*, and you will get a manifestation of love larger than you ever had before. You can say, *I am strength, and power*, and whatever you need.

We are 100 percent human, yes. And we are 100 percent divine. At the intersection of our humanity and divinity, we can claim the power of God and use it to transform our human experience. This is what we seek to realize in prayer through the conscious use of spiritual principle: The transformation of our consciousness so that we may know and live from our divine identity. At the heart of every prayer request, there is either a sense of powerlessness or a desire to celebrate and reinforce just how powerful we are. We seek what we intuitively know is ours innately—spiritual power. Prayer is a process of recognizing and realizing that power, as we access and embody what it means to be divine.

REFLECT AND PRACTICE

๑ How would you explain the prime principle?

๑ When have you experienced oneness? Describe your state of mind during the experience.

๑ Identify occasions when you proved omnipresence, omniscience, and omnipotence.

๑ What happens in your thoughts and feelings when you replace *God is Good* with *God is Goodness*?

๑ What are your arguments for and against believing *God and I are one* or *I am divine*?

CHAPTER 3
Transformative Mind Action

Grounded in human experience, it can be difficult to remember we are also fully divine. The prime principle of oneness can be elusive. This is where affirmative prayer becomes useful because the purpose of prayer is to realize oneness, and the action of prayer is mind transformation. The greatest mind transformation takes place when shifting thoughts from only-human to a divine sense of self, from limited and powerless to infinite and powerful. The effect of prayer is a shift in consciousness. This chapter will examine the spiritual principle of mind action that allows for the first movement of affirmative prayer: *I open to a new understanding.*

What Is Consciousness?

An understanding of consciousness is essential for transformative mind action.

The simplest definition of *consciousness* is awareness or perception. Consciousness includes awareness or perception of our thoughts, emotions, sensations, memories, and knowledge. This definition is incomplete, however, because what we are aware of or perceive is not always apparent. In fact, we operate in varying atmospheres or realms of consciousness.

To say we are *conscious* is to say we are awake, aware, and focused in the present. In a conscious state of being, we can question, contemplate, conclude, and reason based on our recall of knowledge as well as lived experience. Coexisting with all that we consciously recognize is an ocean of *subconscious* thoughts, emotions, beliefs, memories, and knowledge stored but not readily accessible. The subconscious environment includes autonomic bodily processes such as digestion. The most significant feature of the subconscious, though, is a mixture of buried thoughts, emotions, and memories that have congealed into fixed yet unexamined beliefs.

We have learned ways to uncover contents of the subconscious to improve our human condition through self-help and therapy. For students of spirituality an element is missing if we only address our issues at the conscious and subconscious level. We recognize an expansive realm of consciousness that is the point of our divinity, the *superconscious* realm. Charles Fillmore equated the superconscious mind with the "God-man" or divine human. All our spiritual capacities reside in the superconscious or Christ consciousness state of being.

Consciousness is addressed in the third of five principles taught in Unity, which states that we create our life experiences through our way of thinking.

Let's take a moment here to examine the New Thought concept of thinking and thought. In classical New Thought, great emphasis was placed on the cerebral activity of our minds, believing thought informed and created our emotions and beliefs. Science and experience tells us that our cerebral thoughts both inform and are informed by our whole belief system, which is created through the interaction of our thoughts, beliefs, emotions, and somatic experiences. Emotions can create thoughts and vice versa. Our use of the words *thoughts* and *thinking* encompasses this holistic understanding.

One of the organizing principles of New Thought states that we create our life experiences by means of the thoughts held in mind that become beliefs. The consistent, persistent pattern of our beliefs is a truthful predictor of our human experience. When our outlook on life is positive, we tend to notice and therefore experience a positive state of affairs and vice versa.

Thoughts are formative, which means ideas, mental images, and emotions work together. Ideas form mental images that evoke emotions. Mental images trigger thoughts and emotions. Emotions give rise to ideas and mental images. One strengthens and validates the other, leading to further resonant thoughts, mental images, and emotions.

While all thoughts are formative, not all thoughts are creative. Creative thoughts—those leading to an experience or manifestation—are those that are particularly potent; they have been held persistently and/or are backed by strong emotion and conviction. This is true for wanted as well as unwanted thoughts.

Furthermore, the human mind is pivotal in its capacity to distinguish among conscious, subconscious, and superconscious streams of thought. We can acknowledge fully human thoughts and elevate them for a broader outlook. In human terms, *seeing is believing*, but spiritually *believing is seeing*.

Taking to heart that we are capable of transforming our thoughts and beliefs, and noting that affirmative prayer is a tool we can use to transform our thoughts and beliefs, let's look more closely at the creative power of the mind.

Mind Action, the Creative Power

There is one underlying law and ... through this law all things come into expression; also ... there is one universal mind, the source, the sole origin of all real intelligence. First is mind, then mind expresses itself in ideas, then the ideas make themselves manifest.

—Charles Fillmore, *Jesus Christ Heals*

34

Our essential nature is creative. We create our experience, which is to say that all of our thoughts, beliefs, and deep-seated convictions, whether conscious or subconscious, are the raw material from which we create the life we are living.

If we want to know what we truly believe, we can look at our lives. They are an outpicturing of all that we believe. Keep in mind that our experiences are not just a result of our own beliefs but reflect beliefs held by the collective as well (read more about collective consciousness in Chapter 8). All these thoughts, beliefs, and deeply held convictions reflect themselves in our experience and environment, both in our physical body and the larger world of our affairs. If we want to change those experiences, we must be willing to change what we believe.

This is the hallmark of creative mind action: We are in the seat of power. We are the gardener and the architect of our own lives. If we wanted tomatoes but ended up with watermelons, it means we planted watermelon seeds. However, every moment contains the potential for making a new choice. Every moment is ripe with our inherent capacity to transform the very texture of our lives as we choose to plant a different seed. We create by the power of mind action.

Mind, Idea, and Expression

The power of mind action is the creative process at work in the flow of affirmative prayer. The creative process is the way the invisible becomes visible, and the infinite gets expressed in finite ways. It is an orderly progression of mind, idea, and expression, the action of divine order.

Mind is the absolute, the Infinite, oneness. *Mind*, also recognized as divine mind, is the Source of all potentiality. To name it God might simplify it but make it harder to identify with. *Mind* is the prime principle.

Idea is the creative medium. The divine idea is the ideal state of being, the principle or power that can be claimed and embodied. Classical Unity teachings refer to *idea* as the Christ or I AM, meaning Mind's perfect idea. We can infer from this explanation that *idea* is our capacity to recognize and embody divine mind in particular ways.

Expression is manifestation in time and space. *Expression* may include physical manifestation as well as experience and embodiment or capacity to act.

Electricity is an example of how the orderly sequence from invisible to visible works. Electricity is invisible principle that, when activated through a medium, will ultimately manifest as light. The light is an effect, a possible outcome of the activation of something invisible. Electricity can light our homes and it can also be used as the final sentence for death row inmates. The principle is the same; how we choose to use the principle can be vastly different.

The way we choose to activate *Mind* is what defines our uniqueness. Out of infinite potential, we choose. We do not dissolve and disappear into the Divine; we are individualized by our selections. We may consciously use this power to become an ice skater, or a painter, or a thief, or a liar. The choice is always ours.

Just as seeds grow when they are planted in fertile soil, we express the principles and powers that we recognize in *Mind* and nurture as *ideas*.

We are always using divine order, the process of manifestation. Indeed, the heart of affirmative prayer engages the creative process. In the flow of affirmative prayer, we acknowledge oneness, which can be understood as divine mind—all intelligence, all power, and the source of all divine ideas. Starting with concern about an unwanted experience, we recognize a particular divine idea, which is a principle or power, an ideal that can be claimed, realized, and expressed. Claiming oneness, we realize we can therefore express or embody that principle or power in our life, changing our thinking and changing our experience.

Another term for transforming thoughts or shifting consciousness is *healing*.

Healing: The Creative Process and Fulfillment of Prayer

The Unity movement was built upon the founders' healing ministry. The prayer ministry, started in the late 1800s, was often referred to as a healing ministry. Prayer services were labeled healing meetings. Throughout the generations and to this day, whether the request is for inner peace, harmony, prosperity, or health, the true purpose of prayer is healing.

To heal is to claim and realize a spiritual principle by which to restore, to resolve, or to improve our experience. Essentially, to heal is to return to health. The meaning of health, usually defined as freedom from illness or injury, in our understanding, is wholeness (completeness) and well-being in every aspect of life. This principle of health/wholeness includes our bodies, minds, emotions, and spiritual concerns.

Make special note of these two essential teachings about healing:

1) Healing is not a phenomenon that happens *to* us. We heal when we realize a spiritual principle. Take a moment to contemplate this Truth. Maybe you can point to times when healing appeared miraculous or spontaneous.

DeeAnn broke her back when she was 26 years old. In chronic pain, she explored multiple paths of healing. This injury actually ignited her spiritual journey. Through meditation, alternative healing modalities, and deep introspection, the pain eventually disappeared. There were, however, ongoing challenges that arose over the ensuing years due to the physiological shift in the bones in her spine. Then, 31 years after the break, DeeAnn had a spontaneous healing. One day, suddenly, the physiological distortion in her back corrected itself. It was gone. While the healing was spontaneous, it manifested after years of consciousness-building. The healing was evidence of an embodied shift in DeeAnn's consciousness. Her more deeply realized understanding of wholeness resulted in a spontaneous realignment of her spine.

Linda, too, experienced a sudden healing nine years after her father had disowned her. Through those nine years, Linda prepared for reconciliation in her spiritual practice. Although at the time it seemed miraculous, Linda recognized that she had healed her thoughts, mental images, and emotions with regard to her father. She had kept her heart open and ready. Hearing her father's voice for the first time after all those years, and his words of regret and apology, Linda recognized that the circumstances shifted to conform to her consciousness.

As noted below, material resolution does not always occur as part of healing. Even if Linda's father had never reached out to her, if he had died before a chance at reconciliation, Linda healed.

2) Although healing is widely believed to be asso-ciated with curing a condition, a condition does not need to resolve in order for healing to happen. Healing occurs at the level of *Mind*. When we in-ternalize the divine idea or principle of wholeness (or peace, or abundance), we claim the principle in order to embody it. We can then use the prin-ciple to alter our thinking and behavior, healing our experience. When we heal our experience, the

condition is no longer an issue. Whether the condition resolves or not, we are whole, peaceful, or prosperous and we experience the positive effects of the consciousness shift.

A friend diagnosed with multiple sclerosis, experiencing fear and worry about becoming incapacitated, prayed for healing. Recognizing God as the source of wholeness, our friend thought about the nature of wholeness. He thought about the truth of wholeness, the fullness of life, and well-being. He studied the principle. Our friend realized the principle of wholeness by waking up each morning responsive to what he and his body were capable of at the time. He chose to live as well as possible, to consider his life as much more than a diagnosis. He found he could thrive no matter the physical symptoms of the moment. In time, he noticed longer stretches during which he felt well.

Health and wholeness, often used interchangeably in Unity, speak to the totality of emotional, physical, mental, and spiritual well-being. According to Ernest Holmes:

Healing is not a process but a revelation; for the revealing of the perfect man always heals. The process, if there is one, is the time and thought that it takes to arrive at the correct understanding of man's perfect state in Spirit.
—Ernest Holmes, *Science of Mind*

Unity cofounder Charles Fillmore taught that a spiritual realization of the principle of health results from holding in mind a statement of health that satisfies the mind and reassures us of fulfillment. What is the truth of health? Here are some statements of health to dwell upon in prayer:

God is health, the state of well-being that is natural to me regardless of my circumstances.

God is wholeness, therefore I am whole and complete in every moment.

God is life, an ever-flowing vitality, independent of changing conditions. God is the life I AM.

My every thought of divine life builds strength, vigor, and power.

Divine life is my life. Wholeness is my nature, and well-being is my natural state.

Affirmative prayer with healing in mind begins with receptivity and openhearted willingness. At a time and in an environment of calm focus, recite a truth statement, perhaps one of the above. Then reflect on its meaning, seeking to understand it as a truth by which you would alter the way you think and act. You might choose to write your reflections in a journal. Afterward, sit in a state of meditation for a few moments, frequently referred to in Unity as the Silence. In meditation, the power of the Truth may take hold in ways that logic alone cannot accomplish. Returning to conscious thought, consider what actions you might take to live in realization of this Truth. When complete, experience appreciation for new and helpful insights.

To heal when experiencing financial struggle, contemplate the principle of abundance. To heal when worrisome thoughts have kept you awake at night, claim the principle of strength, or faith, or peace. To heal disharmony in relationships, claim the principle of love. To heal past resentments, claim the power of release. To heal lethargy and hesitancy, claim the power of zeal.

The process outlined above mirrors the affirmative prayer flow process. There is a much more detailed exploration of each movement of the prayer flow in Chapter 7. Let's continue to take a deeper look at the principles and tools that are the building blocks of affirmative prayer.

REFLECT AND PRACTICE

⊚ Recall some ways you have fulfilled the creative process. Identify Mind, idea, and expression in each case.

⊚ Recognize one situation or issue in your life that is ripe for healing. Identify one or two principles that you could study and use. Think about how you could use the principle(s) to heal the issue.

⊚ Select one of the health/wholeness affirmations in this chapter to recite as part of your daily spiritual practice this week. At the end of the week, write your insights in a journal or share them with a study partner.

CHAPTER 4

Affirmation and Negation

Affirmative prayer relies upon statements of Truth, or affirmations, as anchors for shifting awareness from powerlessness to empowerment. A complementary tool is negation, or in classical Unity teachings, denial. Negations are statements renouncing false beliefs with their accompanying negative thinking. Both affirmation and negation are essential. Think of them as declaring a wholehearted *yes* and an emphatic *no* when applicable. We begin with the more familiar of the two, affirmation.

The Power of Affirmation

Statements of affirmation are declarations of truth about the spiritual principles and divine ideas we have been exploring in previous chapters. An affirmation's effectiveness, impact, and potency require our activation of the foundational principle of oneness in our life. When spoken from realization of the truth of our divine identity, affirmations are transformative.

And what if you are not yet completely comfortable with the idea of your divine identity? Affirmations are also a powerful tool for evolving our spiritual capacity to know our divine nature by targeting and transforming limiting beliefs. We have all given power to words, thoughts, emotions, and beliefs that do not serve our highest and best. With affirmations, we have the power to transform them.

Writing Affirmations

Here are some simple guidelines for writing effective affirmations:

1. Use first-person, declarative language starting with *I AM*. This is a declaration of your divine identity, also referred to as Christ consciousness, verity consciousness, Buddha consciousness, or Self.

2. Construct affirmations that are short, focused, and easily repeatable. The more direct the affirmation, the more power it will have.

3. Write affirmations in present tense. We are affirming what is true right now, not what we hope eventually will be. Present tense acknowledges this truth.

4. Make the vocabulary personal to you. Use your own manner of speaking. Use words that touch you on a feeling level. For example, notice whether you feel a difference in how each of these words impacts you: *wealthy, rich, prosperous, well-off.* Language reflects consciousness. As we seek to shift our consciousness, exploring language allows us to craft an affirmation that truly speaks to us and furthers transformation.

5. Focus on *what* you are or what you *know* or *can do*, not the *how* or *why*. Affirmations are statements of truth about our divine identity, *what* we are and what we are capable of. *How* or *why* are

human-level concerns that can actually impede realization of our divine identity. We must first know *what* is possible before we can step into *how* it will happen.

When crafting an affirmation, it is important to remember that an affirmation is a statement of Truth. A capital "T" implies that an affirmation is a statement of absolute Truth rather than relative or "my truth." Affirmation is a present-moment Truth about the nature of being rather than a prediction of future behavior. It's about declaring *I AM* in terms of spiritual capacity rather than human characteristics. It's about declaring an accessible truth rather than a desired condition.

Examples of Affirmations

Peace

I AM the living embodiment of perfect peace.
I AM serenity, centered in peace.
I AM peace in the midst of every circumstance.

Love

Today I radiate compassionate love in all I say and do.
I AM a living expression of harmonious love.
I AM the unifying power of love in my relationships.

Wisdom

I live by the illuminating power of wisdom.
I AM divine wisdom, choosing wisely.
I AM the discerning power of wisdom, listening for my next steps.

Power

I AM spiritual power, focused and clear.
I stand in spiritual power with ease and grace.

I AM the power of self-mastery, demonstrating spiritual intelligence.

Prosperity

I AM divine abundance, the power of plenty.
I AM the power of prosperity, giving and receiving gratefully.
I AM and I now demonstrate divine abundance.

Wholeness

I AM the vitality of divine life, whole and healthy.
I AM whole, complete, and wonderfully divine.
I AM well-being, thriving in each moment.

Affirmations Are Not ...

The examples above are all affirmations that are anchored in spiritual principle. Many popular affirmations available through social media are anchored not in our divine identity but in our human experience. Some examples might be:

> *I love myself as I am.*
> *I am healthy, wealthy, and wise.*
> *It's okay not to be okay.*
> *I am proud of myself for getting this far.*
> *I am allowed to say* no *to others and* yes *to myself.*
> *I will be kind to myself and others today.*

Notice that each of the statements listed above reveal relative or "my truth," focus on behavior (*I love ... It's okay ... I am allowed to*), predict future behavior (*I will be*), or declare a desired condition (*I am healthy*).

As motivating as these statements may be, they differ from affirmations as defined by Unity and New Thought. To be clear, saying any form of encouraging statements to ourselves is beneficial, and we would want everyone freely and frequently to tell themselves of their essential goodness as well as to envision ideal circumstances. But to clarify further, affirmations are different from positive thinking. Positive thinking is optimism. Optimism is a general state of positivity about our human condition.

Unity and New Thought affirmations are not:

◉ Positive thinking—optimism *(Every day I'm getting better and better; things have a way of turning out right; it's all good.)*

◉ Possibility thinking—chances are ... *(I know there's a better-fitting job; the employer I am seeking is seeking me.)*

◉ Wishful thinking—magical thinking *(I am a millionaire.)*

An effective affirmation is not wishful or magical thinking and not a prediction of a resolution; rather, it is a statement of what is true here and now. Here is an example for how we might use an affirmation when in bed with the flu, an example that is accessible and not anchored in our human experience:

> *Divine life is my true state of being. Every cell in my body is thrumming with divine life.*

Affirming we are divine life while wracked with chills and body aches can be challenging. Our human experience can dominate our awareness anytime we are attempting a shift in consciousness. An old understanding, perhaps that this flu has to simply run its course before I get better, can impede our capacity to center in and realize Truth in the moment.

As you gain in your practice of affirmation, check your statements in light of the guidelines above for greatest effectiveness.

Effects of Practicing Affirmation

Affirmations, as defined for affirmative prayer, have definite effects in consciousness. Especially when counteracting nega-

tive patterns of thinking, affirmations recondition consciousness and connect our human identity to our divine identity.

**Affirmations increase our ability to anchor Truth as our real-
ity.** "Each affirmation helps to build up a substantial, firm,
unwavering state of mind, because it establishes Truth in consciousness." (Charles Fillmore, *Keep a True Lent*)

Affirmations change our biochemistry. "We quicken our life
by affirming that we are alive with the life of Spirit; our intelligence by affirming our oneness with divine intelligence; and we
quicken the indwelling, interpenetrating substance by recognizing and claiming it as our own." (Charles Fillmore, *Prosperity*)

Affirmations lead to spiritual realization. "Affirming a statement will not make it so because you affirm it; but if the statement is true to principle, then affirming it will help to make it
as true for you personally as it is true universally." (Charles Fillmore, *Atom-Smashing Power of Mind*)

An affirmation is a declaration of spiritual Truth, supporting us in the way an anchor holds a boat steady in its position
on the water. An affirmation is a claim on Truth, our demand on
Truth to establish itself in mind and heart.

Working with Affirmations

We suggest saturating your awareness with select affirmations until they become second nature. Place them everywhere
you are likely to see them—around your house, car, or office.
Record them and play them while driving, doing dishes, or at
other times. Write them 10 to 20 times daily. Say them aloud
as often as you can each day, emphatically and enthusiastically.
If the words or tone do not feel right to you, restate them until
they do.

The Power of Negation

So what do we do when we truly cannot center in Truth? When our human experience is so loud and so present we cannot authentically affirm our divine nature?

Just as we can affirm Truth to shift our consciousness, we can negate false beliefs to shift our consciousness. Negation is our term for *denial* in classical New Thought. The word *denial* has taken on a widespread psychological meaning in our world today, one that implies disbelief that something is happening, the proverbial sticking your head in the sand. That is not the intent behind New Thought denial. To us, *negation* is a clearer term than *denial*, avoiding any confusion regarding this powerful practice.

Negations use the great *no* power of our awareness. They activate our ability to release and let go of beliefs that no longer serve. Negations support our power to refuse or reject. Negations are a conscious choice to remove power from an old thought or belief, disrupting them from manifesting in ways we no longer wish to experience.

Practicing negation is a way we can meet our humanness with Truth. Our divine nature is more powerful than our human perspective, as scripture points out so eloquently by actually using a powerful negation: "The words that I say to you I do not speak on my own; but the Father who dwells in me does his works" (John 14:10 RSV). Jesus meant it is not our human-only consciousness but our divine identity that is leading the way.

Just as affirmations are not wishing or hoping something will happen, negations similarly are not wishing or hoping something will go away. Negations are not pretending that something is not happening because it makes us uncomfortable.

Negation, as we are using the word, cannot happen on a surface level. Negations require a decision and a deep realization that a belief or thought is false so that any correlated feelings can be transformed. It is an attempt to neutralize the creative energy around a negative belief, to create an absence so the old beliefs no longer have any power.

By negation we do not mean suppression. We do not mean ignoring the challenges in our life, which would be considered spiritual bypass. Spiritual bypass is a short-circuit around something that is seeking to be healed by pretending it isn't really there. We are so uncomfortable about facing something that we go around rather than straight through to the very heart of it.

In order to step into authentic negation, we must first admit and recognize our present state of affairs. This includes "what is" right now and also how we feel and think about "what is" right now. We then choose to release false beliefs that have contributed to our current feelings. To do this we must go through a process of self-realization. Negations do not repress false beliefs, they release them. We never negate facts or the feelings arising from the facts.

We negate the power of:

- Beliefs we harbor about the permanence of our circumstance or the length of time it is taking to resolve.

- Negative interpretations of the circumstances, such as making it mean that something is missing, wrong, or broken in our life.

- Identification with the condition, like naming it "my" disease or making the condition a bigger part of our life than it actually is.

- Believing what I have been told and what "everyone" knows about our condition. This is known as collective consciousness, such as claiming seasonal allergies because "everyone" has them.

- Self-punishing beliefs about God and human nature, perhaps that we are not worthy or deserving of abundance, well-being, and joy.

Here is an example of a potent negation, based upon and paraphrased from Charles Fillmore in *Jesus Christ Heals:*

> *I deny that I inherit any belief that in any way could limit my health, intelligence, or power to do good.* There is no external authority that could convince me I am unworthy or unable. I am now free from every assumption that could interfere with my capacity to be healthy, prosperous, peaceful, and wise.

We meet false beliefs with a gentle negation. Negations are not forceful because their intention is not to add any energy to the thoughts and beliefs that no longer serve us.

Practicing Negation and Affirmation Together

Negations are most powerful when paired with affirmations. First, we neutralize and release the old or false belief, then we activate and embrace a new idea or Truth. When feeling afraid about the future, for example, we may gently say something like:

> *I give no power to fear. I am faith in action and step forward confidently. I release any power or energy around feeling stuck. I know I AM limitless potential and that new possibilities are available right now.*

The power of working with negations and affirmations is that you can truly acknowledge where you are. You can be honest with yourself about what you are experiencing and meet yourself with Truth. Negations are incredibly empowering as they literally are saying: *I choose where to give my power and I choose to place it here, not there.*

In our example earlier of having the flu, affirmations and negations might be paired together like this:

I give no power to this disease. Divine life is my true state of being. I release any attachment to how long healing takes. Every cell in my body is thrumming with divine life right now.

In this example, we are acknowledging and negating the story that the flu is in charge and deciding the impact on our body temple. We are instead activating our capacity to be divine life and that it is present and available right now.

Use the following worksheet to facilitate your practice of affirmations and negations. To master them is to master the heart of affirmative prayer. Take time to work with these essential building blocks and deepen your own awareness of Truth. In the following chapters we will be applying these powerful statements of Truth to the affirmative prayer process.

REFLECT AND PRACTICE

⊚ Review the affirmations you wrote in Chapter 1 in light of the instruction in this chapter. Edit them according to the guidelines.

⊚ Reviewing the effects of practicing affirmation, share your insights from practicing affirmations this past week.

⊚ Bring to mind an issue you want to heal. Follow the Negation and Affirmation Practice on the next page to arrive at an affirmation you can live into this week.

⊚ Now that you have written an affirmation, how do you imagine living into it during the week ahead? The more specific and actionable, the more powerful. For example, you could pledge to devote the first 15 minutes of each morning to repeating the affirmation and imagining using it in the appointments you have today.

Negation and Affirmation Practice

Condition (concise phrase, for example: *my house is not selling*, or *my brother is ill and I am worried*, or *I am having trouble with my ex*).

_____

_____

Facts (two or three facts, not suppositions, judgments, or conclusions). We do not deny what is happening.

_____

_____

I feel (for example: insecure; fearful; worthless). We do not deny feelings.

_____

_____

What I believe about the condition now (about God, self, life, what is possible or impossible).

_____

_____

I negate (release, eliminate, erase, renounce, reject, refuse, stop, relinquish, say *no* to) the false beliefs.

_____

_____

I affirm (I claim, I AM—statements of being from your divine identity).

_____

_____

Review your affirmation. Is it present tense, an absolute rather than relative statement, and does it have personally meaningful language?

I promise to live the affirmation. (*Now that I know my divine identity, I will* ... —statements of "doing" that are clear and measurable)

_____

_____

CHAPTER 5
Recognize the Nature of God

We have defined affirmative prayer. We have identified the prime principle, which is oneness. We have examined the power of mind action to shift thought. Each of these principles support the movements of affirmative prayer. Our second movement, God Is, is what we will be focusing upon next as we grapple with our understanding of God. Why attempt to define God? Because our understanding of God determines the way we pray.

Our understanding of God has evolved over time, both collectively and individually. We evolve our God consciousness by paying attention to what we were taught to believe and what we are being invited to understand now.

As we have discussed in the opening chapters, God is not a being, but *beingness*. And yet for so many of us, our understanding of God is rooted in our humanness. Ken Wilber, an American philosopher who developed his own integral theory, offers a powerful model to examine our understanding of God within the human experience.

With his Three Faces of God concept, Wilber has identified how we, from our human experience, view and understand the nature of God. As Unity and New Thought do not subscribe to an anthropomorphized deity with faces, for clarity we will name how we identify and understand God as the Three Perspectives of God.

Three Perspectives of God

Three perspectives or views on God can be understood in the language we use to identify God. Do we call God an *it*? Speak to God as *you*? Realize God as *I*? Each perspective offers us something slightly different.

It is. When we understand God as a transcendent, exterior, objective phenomenon, we are *recognizing God*. We may recognize God as the infinite cosmos, presence, the absolute, divine principle, the Universe, Spirit, or infinite allness. We can experience a reaction to this transcendent God, like awe or connection. "It" is something we recognize, name, and describe.

Most faith traditions have some aspect of recognizing God as an exterior phenomenon that can be reflected upon—the God we talk *about*. As we have seen in our opening chapter on the prime principle, this perspective in Unity and New Thought—that God can be recognized—is foundational to what we teach and know.

You are. When we understand God as a shared, relational experience, we are *relating to God*. We may relate to God as the beloved, mirror self, Buddha, Kwan Yin, or Jesus. Many people relate to God as presence, which is a personal experience of the power of God that can also be experienced as intimacy between ourselves and others. In this way of understanding presence, it is a feeling of connection. The late Unity minister Sky St. John spoke of "God with skin on."

Most traditional religions relate to God as a deity or entity that is prayed to and who cares for us, often within a parent/child relationship. This is the God we talk *with*. In Unity and New Thought we do not pray to a deity that we consider outside of us. Our relating to God is instead how we see and relate to the divinity we experience within ourselves and others. Each person we meet is an opportunity to relate to and interact with the Divine. It is this relational understanding of God that invites us to be in service, to pray with others, and to connect.

I AM. When we understand God as immanent, an interior, subjective experience within, we are *realizing God*. We may realize God as the I AM, the Silence, or Christ/Buddha consciousness. This realization means there is no separation. There is only oneness.

Many mystical aspects of the world's faith traditions are anchored in realizing God as immanent, an interior experience. This is the I we *are*. In Unity and New Thought, realizing *I AM* fuels the power and impact of affirmative prayer. It is how we claim, activate, and inhabit what we recognize about God. It is how we move from a God we talk about to standing in our divine identity. We will be exploring in Chapter 6 how we claim this as our true nature.

Prayer can include any and all of the three perspectives of God explained above. There is no wrong way to pray. Ultimately, the prime principle of oneness invites us to hold all three perspectives: God as a transcendent, exterior, objective experience; God as the experience of one another; and God as an immanent, interior, subjective experience. Notice where you orient naturally and practice opening to the perspectives less familiar and perhaps less comfortable to you. Evolving God consciousness is always about a larger understanding.

Bring to mind the words you choose to describe God. Think about how you speak about God, qualities you identify with God, and characteristics of the nature of God. Write them in a list. Next, review your list with these questions in mind:

- Which words on your list refer to God as a distinctive being such as Father, Mother, Compassionate One, or Great Spirit?

- Which refer to God in the abstract, such as All That Is or the Universe?

- Which describe God (by any name) as an actor, such as healer or protector?

- Which identify God as a characteristic that you could relate to and imagine being able to embody, such as love, strength, peace, or wisdom?

As we examine various approaches to understanding the nature of God, notice points of agreement and disagreement, acceptance and resistance. In our estimation, wrestling with our understanding of God leads us to a greater God, a God we can identify with. When our grasp on God expands, our prayer leads to expanded consciousness.

Principles

Defining the nature of God in terms of principles provides the means for us to recognize the principles within and to identify ourselves as divine. It promotes our ability to claim, realize, actualize, and embody the nature of God, fulfilling the prime principle of oneness.

God Is Principle

We have established that God is prime principle. To fulfill the promise of affirmative prayer, it's essential to recognize that God is principle. We cannot state it any more clearly than it appears in *Jesus Christ Heals* by Charles Fillmore:

> The fundamental basis and starting point of practical Christianity is that God is principle. By principle is meant definite, exact, and unchangeable rules of action ... From the teaching that the Deity is a person, we have come to believe that God is changeable; that He gets angry with His people and condemns them; that some are chosen or favored before others; that in His sight good and evil are verities, and that He defends the

one and deplores the other. We must relieve our minds of these ideas of a personal God ruling over us in an arbitrary, manlike manner.

God is mind. Mind evolves ideas. These ideas evolve in an orderly way. The laws of mind are just as exact and undeviating as the laws of mathematics or music. To recognize this is the starting point to finding God.

At this point, you may be thinking it would be simpler to drop the word *God* altogether. The Unity founders struggled with the same idea:

Sometimes I think it is unwise to put that word "God" in, because it carries to our minds the idea of an arbitrary being that will bring us things.
—Charles Fillmore, "The Enduring Nature of Love,"
Sunday, August 3, 1930

God is neither male nor female, but principle. God is not a cold, senseless principle like that of mathematics, but the principle of life, love, and intelligence.
—Myrtle Fillmore, *How to Let God Help You*

Language can be a powerful doorway into our beliefs. Within words and phrases entire belief structures exist, revealing embedded theology. Embedded theology consists of religious education, ideas, and understandings that we have absorbed so that they are embedded unconsciously, often so deeply we don't readily recognize them. They dwell in the subconscious mind.

The word *God* can trigger our embedded theology. It means different things to different people, generally reflecting an anthropomorphized deity that, as Charles Fillmore expressed above, is often seen as being an expression of us—our foibles, our shortcomings, our desires all amplified in an all-powerful being. God is not an expression of us. Rather, we are an expression of the Divine. To highlight this, a variety of alternate words for God are widely used to shift understanding away from anthropomorphism. Some other terms for God are: principle, life, love, oneness, wholeness, First Cause, divine mind, Truth, the absolute, the Tao, isness, beingness, divine consciousness, the Universe, Spirit, Great Spirit, divine presence, unified field, quantum consciousness, infinite allness, the thing itself, light, love, intelligence, universal mind, and the cosmos.

Look back at the list you wrote at the start of this chapter and you will find numerous alternatives to the word *God*. Many of them are principles such as love, wisdom, peace, and strength.

Thinking of God as principle instead of person prepares the way for us to claim our divine identity. According to Charles Fillmore:

> God is not like a man; God is omnipresent Spirit,
> accessible just like electricity, just like sunshine,
> just like air, to your mind, your thought.
> —Charles Fillmore, "The Undisciplined States of
> Consciousness," Sunday, April 12, 1931

Recognizing Principles

Out of the prime principle, oneness, we can identify numerous principles that describe the nature of God in particularity. It's as if the prime principle is the atmosphere, invisible yet populated with particles that can be identified, understood, and used. For example, omnipresence is the principle of pervasiveness and simultaneity. When we recognize God as source and substance, in all and through all, and when we realize every needed resource is within us in all places and at all times, we are proclaiming omnipresence. From the principle of omnipresence, other principles can be known, such as order, abundance, and wholeness.

To reiterate the definition of principle from Chapter 2, a principle is a fact or a constant that has no opposite and is values-neutral. A principle is an invisible or intangible truth that becomes visible in our expression of it. A principle is an absolute that can be expressed relatively.

The Absolute and the Relative

Absolute Truth, or spiritual principle, becomes known in relative or human experience. Another way to say this is that behind all that is visible lies an invisible principle. Principle is not something we can see or touch, but we can see evidence of the principles of love, joy, and peace all around us. Principles undergird all that is in the relative or manifest realm. They are not based in circumstances, but we demonstrate principles in human circumstances. A few examples might be helpful.

Order is an absolute principle. Order is the principle of organization, adjustment, and evolution. We demonstrate order relatively when we clean and organize a physical space, when we schedule calendar appointments, or in the progression from our college application all the way through to an earned academic degree. Order is not imposed upon us but is ours to claim and demonstrate.

Beauty is an absolute principle. Beauty is the principle of recognizing and responding to the essential essence of something we behold. Charles Fillmore said, "The idea back of the flower is beauty" (*Mysteries of Genesis*). In the relative world, we may use the word *beauty*, though we have arbitrarily linked it to specific characteristics that we say makes something beautiful. If those criteria are not met, instead of beauty we label someone or something pretty, average, plain, or ugly. None of these are absolutes. They are adjectives describing a human understanding and value system. They are changeable depending on culture and personal preferences.

Notice the distinction between saying to yourself, *I am beautiful* or *I am beauty*. The former is a value judgment and has an opposite—*I am ugly*. *I am beauty* as an absolute principle has no opposite. Our capacity to embody beauty empowers us to discover the rich essence of everyone and everything, regardless of cultural constructs.

12 Powers, Many Principles

Each of the 12 powers as taught by Unity is a familiar quality in human expression. Each is also a spiritual principle, absolute and immutable. Each power/principle describes an aspect of the nature of God in terms we can recognize, relate to, and identify as our true nature.

The 12 powers or principles all spring from the prime principle, oneness. All powers are inherent, yet all powers are latent. They exist in potential and need to be developed, cultivated, claimed, and embodied to be useful.

When developed, cultivated, claimed, and realized through spiritual practice, the principles inherent in the powers support our most inspired spiritual living. The 12 powers are:

Faith: perception, conviction, expectancy

Understanding: comprehension, realization, insight

Will: choice, commitment, willingness

Imagination: conception, vision, embodiment

Zeal: enthusiasm, audacity, devotion

Power: concentration, self-mastery, authority

Love: magnetism, harmony, unity

Wisdom: judgment, discernment, intuition

Strength: stability, courage, tenacity

Order: organization, adjustment, evolution

Release/Negation: cleansing, renunciation, repentance

Life: animation, vitality, presence

The discussion of spiritual principles often gives rise to questions about qualities and attributes not explicit in the 12 powers or the three *omnis*. Is joy a principle? Peace? Abundance? Wholeness? Justice? Beauty? Yes! We can recognize in each of these principles an absolute and immutable Truth independent of particular circumstances. They have no opposites except in relative use.

God Is a Useful Principle

We have reflected on our understanding of the nature of God. We have broadened our definitions to include spiritual principles. Now we have a useful God, a useful set of principles.

The more we study spiritual principles, including the 12 powers, the more readily we recognize them and use them in prayer and in daily living. When we recognize and activate spiritual principles, we claim them as our own. We fulfill the prime principle, oneness. We become more and more able to use invisible, absolute principles, demonstrating them in human experience. This is an essential part of affirmative prayer, recognizing *God is* and making it useful.

REFLECT AND PRACTICE

- How do you understand the three perspectives of God? Which perspective feels the most challenging? Why?

- Reflect on the word *God*. What comes to mind? What images, feelings, ideas do you connect with that word?

  - Think about your childhood understanding of God. What did you believe? How did you understand God then?

  - Think about your understanding of God now. What do you believe now? How do you understand God now?

  - What would you like to believe? What new understanding would you like to explore and experience?

  - What are the words that you currently use for *God*?

  - What are some new words that speak to you or that you are willing to explore?

- Identify two or three personal prayer needs/intentions/requests. Write one or more *God is* ... statements for each.

- ๑ Review your statements for an indication of God as a personality/person.

- ๑ Does your statement recognize a principle (noun) rather than an action (verb)?

- ๑ Are you describing being rather than doing? Example: *God is love* rather than *God is loving.*

CHAPTER 6
Claim Divine Identity

Recognizing the nature of God as principle, we can claim the principle as our own. We claim the spiritual authority of *I AM*, by which we become able to heal, to thrive, and to manifest the life we deeply desire. This is the third movement of affirmative prayer: *I Integrate I AM*.

I AM, the Divine Human

I AM is our spiritual name when declared in a state of spiritual realization. Known in New Thought as God consciousness or Christ consciousness and taught by Charles Fillmore as the God-man or true spiritual human, "The *I AM* is the metaphysical name of the spiritual self, as distinguished from the human self" (*The Revealing Word*).

In his classic New Thought text on prayer, *The Universe Is Calling*, Unity minister Eric Butterworth instructed:

> When people heard Jesus saying, "I am the light of the world," they thought he was referring to himself, that he was announcing that he was God,

or God's special agent. But he was simply affirming the truth, or "throwing the switch." And he made it clear that each of us must also affirm the truth.

The true affirmation is: *I AM.*

When declaring I AM within spiritual practice, we are acting from spiritual authority, activating spiritual power. We are enacting the law of mind action, dwelling upon Truth so intently that every dimension of being realizes it. The greatest mind action is to pivot away from a sense of ourselves as only human and toward an awareness of our divine identity. This is not to leave our human identity behind but to integrate our divine human. In the affirmative prayer flow, integration is the prayerful acknowledgment of I AM, a moment of enlightened awareness that the spiritual principle recognized is one and the same as I AM.

We are fully human, yes, this we acknowledge, and we are fully divine. We affirm *I AM that* ... (that principle we have recognized as the nature of God).

The Claim of I AM

The I AM teachings are a hallmark of Unity. We consider this so important that it is worth a deeper exploration.

Now we all accept that there is one universal spirit, and I am the offspring of that spirit. That is equivalent to saying, I am Jehovah, or I am Christ ... We are beginning to find that just to the extent that we come to a realization of this Christ in us do we demonstrate it, and you begin your demonstration wherever you are. You can take it in small bites. You can say, I am life, and you will get life; you can say, I am love, and you will get a manifestation of love larger than you ever had before. You can say, I am strength, and power, and whatever you need.

—Charles Fillmore article typewritten and dated April 15, 1923

Notice in this passage Fillmore mentions: "just to the extent that we come to a realization of this Christ in us ..." To say *I AM* and to mean *I am Christ* is in many circles blasphemy! Understandably, to say *I am Christ* or *I am God* is big; it's hard to swallow. That is why we would never say, and we believe Fillmore never said out loud, "I am Christ" or "I am God."

What Fillmore did say is that we can "come to a realization," which is like saying, "awaken to the spiritual reality" of our Christ nature. Through practices such as prayer, meditation, and study, we "take it in small bites." We build upon an expanding consciousness of spiritual integration.

What does it mean to realize and demonstrate I AM? Fillmore leaned into the 12 powers, our spiritual capacities, as descriptors of the indescribable Divine. Each of the powers is a principle within the prime principle, oneness. To reiterate the challenge of claiming I AM, it's easier to say, *I am love* than to say *I am God*. It is also more specific to identify with love as our true nature, to experience and demonstrate love. Some examples:

God is love. Therefore, I AM love. I embody the harmonizing power of love with my coworker.

God is the source of my strength. I AM spiritual strength standing strong and steady in the midst of changing conditions.

God is order. I AM order, by which I organize, adjust, and evolve.

God is beauty. I AM beauty, by which I meet everyone and everything with the delight of discovery.

Notice the progression in these statements: first, recognizing the nature of God as an absolute, or principle; second, identifying with the principle, accepting our rightful *I AM* claim; and third, realizing a way to actualize the principle in relative circumstances. This is the heart of affirmative prayer.

Some schools of metaphysics suggest we ought to say, *I am wealthy* at a time when the bank account is drained or *I am healthy* while experiencing distressing physical symptoms. The rationale is that we believe our way to the desired circumstances.

This approach, a.k.a. "fake it 'til you make it," may have some value, although notice how it is tied to a desired result. Instead of *I am wealthy*, I can more effectively affirm:

> *I AM prosperity, by which I thrive, live well, and recognize an abundance of possibilities.*

I AM is for right now, regardless of the present condition of my wallet. Instead of *I am healthy*, I can affirm:

> *I AM life, celebrating the flow, vitality, and intelligence in every dimension of my being.*

Shifting focus away from outcome and toward enduring principle, I strengthen the life faculty in my body by affirming it now, as my body heals.

The prime principle, oneness, can be a challenging Truth to actualize. God and I are one: a truth easier to proclaim than to claim.

Challenges of Claiming I AM

Our relative human minds have no grasp on oneness. We like the thought of oneness, maybe have periodic mystical moments when we experience oneness. However, we struggle with the idea of oneness, full of arguments against it. We grieve over the loss of a deity God. We believe that were we to claim *I AM*, we would denounce our human self or we would fear being labeled blasphemous. Unable to imagine ourselves being All That Is, we believe we are none of it. Charles Fillmore emphasized that we can rightfully claim our divine identity.

> It is your mission to express all that you can imagine God to be. Let this be your standard of achievement; never lower it, nor allow yourself to be belittled by the cry of sacrilege. You can attain to everything you can imagine. If you can imagine that it is possible to God, it is also possible to you.
> —Charles Fillmore, *Talks on Truth*

From Losing God to Using God

As we expand our understanding of God, we may feel as though we have lost our God. The God we lose is the deity we were taught to love and fear, the deity who would reward and punish, endanger and rescue us. Frankly, while we may not miss the downside of God, we may grieve the loss of a deity we imagined was always looking out for us, loving and protecting, warning us of trouble ahead and swooping us out of it when we had not listened.

When we let go of that God, or our understanding of God in that way, we begin to claim responsibility for our divine humanity. We take to heart the prime principle, oneness, and admit that God and I are one. Here's one way to think about it:

God is love. Not a loving deity. Love itself. The power, the principle love. God, the principle of love, is not a separate, sentient being behaving in human ways. God, the principle of love, is the invisible, absolute Truth, the love within us and all around us. In the state of oneness, we can claim the principle, affirm *I AM love*, recognizing love within our being. As divine humans,

71

we act in relative circumstances, which means we can be loving, we can love, and we can experience love. Acts of love become visible demonstrations of the principle of love that I AM.

God is the stabilizing power of strength, the principle of stability. We can claim: *I AM the stabilizing power of strength.* Instead of relying upon a deity to do something to strengthen us, we can realize oneness and use the principle of stability to remain steady during times of change and uncertainty. We can stabilize our thoughts that had been swirling in confusion.

In both of the examples above, we claim and embody the principle of stability. Reverse the statement: *God, use me.* Say instead *I use Godness.* Instead of *I am an expression of God*, say *God is not expressing me; I express Godness.* Shift away from passive *vessel consciousness*; God and divine principles are not passively flowing through you. Be direct and place the divine human in the seat of action: *I AM expressing spiritual qualities, powers, and principles. I AM embodying spiritual power.* It takes our divine human consciousness to display any and every principle.

As previously addressed, sometimes the word *God* gets in the way of claiming divine identity. If using the word *God* keeps you from claiming *I AM*, you can skip directly to the principle. Instead of *God is love and I AM love*, you can say, *Love is divine and I AM divine love.*

When grieving the thought that you have lost your God, recognize that you have not lost at all; you have gained knowledge of your inherent capacity. Be still and know, in spiritual practice. Remember, you are not a dependent child of the Divine; you are a mature, spiritual being able to internalize and express all that you can imagine God to be.

From Victim Consciousness to Empowerment

It might be helpful at this time to look at the evolution of consciousness. In New Thought, it is described as the four levels of evolving consciousness. There is no wrong in any of these levels—they are each a necessary part of our personal and collective evolution and growth. At its heart, affirmative prayer is a process of empowerment. It offers us an opportunity to realize and stand in our spiritual authority. It is a process that awakens us to our divine nature, healing victim consciousness.

Victim Consciousness: To Me

In victim consciousness we think and feel as if everything is happening *to us*. It is fear-focused. There are external forces at work that are doing things or not doing things that impact our lives. This is the stage where we often say, "Why me?" There is a powerlessness to this consciousness. As we shed our sense of victimhood, we are invited to understand our innate worth and value by releasing shame and blame.

Manifester/Victor Consciousness: By Me

Manifester or victor consciousness is empowering, especially as it arises in response to victim consciousness. In manifester consciousness tools like affirmations and affirmative prayer begin to access the innate, creative power that is ours. There is a sense of control and empowerment, although this stage is also fear-based. We are afraid of being the victim again. This stage can also be called the manipulator, as we can become so focused on controlling our external world, on being victorious, that we lose sight of our own evolving consciousness. Our manifesting/manipulating can become limited by our need to satisfy our small, egocentric self. To move beyond the manifester, we are invited to release our egoic focus on control and power.

Channel/Vessel Consciousness: Through Me

Channel or vessel consciousness is an awareness that something is happening through you. A power guides and informs you. The small understanding of your personality gives way to the awareness of something larger than you. You are the vessel through which God, the Divine, speaks, acts, and makes itself known. There is openness and willingness to learn and to grow. This stage is faith-based, not fear-based. There is still a sense of separation here—author Eric Butterworth said people speak of "God within" like a raisin in a bun. People in channel consciousness use language like, "Something came over me and made me ..." "I made a space and God showed up." "God's will, not my will." "God will do the work." Moving beyond channel consciousness is an invitation to release separation and ego.

Beingness/Christ/Buddha/I AM/Verity Consciousness: As Me

In this state of consciousness, all sense of separation falls away. There is no *me* separate from God. There is only the I AM. This is the opportunity to experience limitless consciousness. There is only total faith. People in this advanced, awakened state renounce all sense of self—even an enlightened self.

While the descriptions above seem to imply this is a linear process, it isn't. Our growth and evolution are additive and inclusive. We always carry within us the stages that preceded where we are now. This is why in times of stress we often feel as if we have regressed. The illustration below can give you a better sense of how we live with these different stages of spiritual awareness.

These levels of consciousness nest like Russian dolls and they are all available to us at any time. Different forms of prayer reflect these levels of consciousness. What makes affirmative prayer so transformative is that the affirmative prayer process doesn't simply reflect where we are, but invites us to move through these stages of evolving consciousness and speak, claim, and live as the I AM. We are provided a path out of victim consciousness and into divine empowerment.

Integrating the Divine Human

Early New Thought writers distinguish the human self as lower, inferior, or mortal compared with the spiritual self or I AM. For them, the human self is in need of reformation or redemption, an unintelligent identity needing education and enlightenment. Contemporary readers might get the impression that the human self is to be sacrificed for the spiritual self or denounced as sinful and unredeemable. This idea shows up in teachings that advocate slaying the ego.

We advocate a more compassionate understanding of being human. Conscious mind and conscious awareness, an intact human identity, is an essential basis for spiritual understanding. We get that human mind and awareness can be deluded, convinced of its supremacy. The teachings promise that spiritual practice leads to integration. The human self in service to the spiritual self, or divine human, sits in the seat of spiritual power.

Teaching about being born anew, or gaining spiritual realization, Charles Fillmore emphasized:

> Man, on the positive, formative, creative side of his nature, is the direct emanation of his Maker; that he is just like his Maker; that he is endowed with creative power, and that his very being is involved in God-Mind, which he is releasing by his creative thought.—*Christian Healing*

Here is another way to conceptualize the integration of human and divine. If the impulse is to ask God to provide something for you, for example peace of mind, you can instead claim peace as your nature, for *I AM one*. You can stand in peace, in the seat of power. God is the invisible, the unformed. God cannot act in the world the way you can. You are the actor in this field. God is peace and you are peace and you can express peace.

When mystics proclaim we are here to be the hands and feet of God, we believe they mean we are to be visible evidence of invisible power. It's not enough just to say that God acts through me—placing myself one-off from God, as if God is doing it and I am merely the hollow flute that God plays through. My consciousness—my ego—is required. My ego is to be in service to my divine identity. That is how we integrate human and divine, and that is how we actualize oneness.

From All or None to One

Sometimes we get right up to the edge of our divine identity. We say *I am a part of God. I am a drop of water in the ocean. I am a piece of God.* Or, passively stated, *God expresses in, through, and as me.* We find our throat closing around the Truth of *I AM divine.*

Because we cannot actualize God or embody all of God, we may back away from being *any* aspect of God. We say *I cannot be that!* However, the fact that I cannot be all God does not mean I cannot be *one* aspect of the nature of God at any point in time.

We only need one aspect of the nature of God, one principle, in any moment. Think about a prayer concern you have, a personal intention or challenge. Ask yourself, *What do I want to know about the nature of God related to this situation?* What aspect of God or spiritual principle would be a remedy for this prayer concern and therefore beneficial for me in this situation?

For example, when searching for your next place of employment, you could recognize the principle of divine imagination. Claim your ability to conceive a divine idea about employment, to envision a full picture of the idea fulfilled, and to embody that idea now by thinking and feeling from the endpoint.

When worrying about money, recognize the principle of spiritual strength and claim it. Using and embodying strength, stabilize your thoughts in abundance consciousness, courageously express appreciation for this moment's bounty, and embody tenacity, the principle of persistence that implies a nonanxious state of keep on keeping on.

During a time of uncertainty or chaotic circumstances, recognize the principle of order. Claim order and use the principle of organization, by which you place your thoughts and actions in order. Using the principle of adjustment, remain flexible and agile. Using the principle of evolution, stay alert for opportunities to think fresh thoughts and move into inspired action.

From Blasphemy to Truth

In the quotation at the start of this section, Charles Fillmore anticipates the pushback from the collective consciousness to the claim of I AM. In essence, he says, don't worry about it! Don't worry that Western culture proclaims humanity's sinfulness, weakness, and helplessness. Don't worry that well-meaning friends might ask, "Who do you think you are? God?"

Rightfully, who are we *not* to claim our spiritual nature, to deny ourselves a complete sense of self? To deny the spiritual self is like denying the air we breathe, invisible yet essential.

We are in favor of reminding ourselves frequently that we are 100 percent human and 100 percent divine—a divine human.

> If you are looking at yourself, or any other man, in any way but as the God man, you are really lying to yourself about yourself or others.
>
> —Charles Fillmore, unpublished,
> *Releasing the Holy Spirit of Man*, Lesson 3

Why is this so important? It is from the I AM that we can realize what else is possible. It is from this integrated awareness that we discover what is ours to do, to know, to have, or to understand in a new way. It is from the I AM that we ultimately realize how we can demonstrate and manifest the I AM in time and space. This is an essential movement in affirmative prayer, the integration of the I AM.

The Realization of *I Can*

Having recognized the nature of God as principle and power, we claim I AM, integrating human and divine consciousness. These two movements in the affirmative prayer process reveal spiritual power always present and poised for our demonstration in our relative or human circumstances. The prayer flow now naturally moves into the fourth movement, *I recognize I can, I have, I know,* where we realize what it means to demonstrate spiritual power in our life.

> Realization precedes demonstration. A realization
> is the fulfillment in mind of an idea before there is
> a manifestation.
> —Charles Fillmore, *Jesus Christ Heals*,
> Lesson 3 archived notes, May 1, 1940

Recall the flow of mind action from Chapter 3: Mind, idea, and expression. Notice that we recognize Mind (spiritual principle or power), claim idea (divine identity), and then manifest. Flowing from idea to expression requires realization. Realization is the awareness of what becomes possible because God is ... and *I AM* ... therefore I can ...

> Spiritual realization changes things. In scientific
> prayer, realization is the high point of attainment.
> With concentrated spiritual attention, man can
> affirm in faith that God spirit is present and that
> he, man, is one with the God presence.
> —Charles Fillmore,
> *Atom-Smashing Power of Mind*

Realization is a practical, logical movement from conceptualization to actualization. The question in realization is: What can I now do or have or know to focus my attention? What change can I make in the way I choose to think or act to cooperate with Truth and embody the principle or power claimed in prayer?

For example, when recognizing God as the harmony of divine love and claiming *I AM harmony*, how might I begin thinking differently about the altercation I had with my neighbor? How might I embody harmony in thought and behavior?

When recognizing God as understanding and claiming *I AM understanding*, what might I change about the content and quality of my thoughts in this situation? How might I embody understanding in my next steps?

Myrtle Fillmore taught:

> God is life; we make that life into living. God
> is love; we make divine love into loving. God is
> substance; we take the substantial reality and
> bring it through into the manifest world. God is
> wisdom; we claim oneness with divine wisdom
> and it expresses through us as wise thoughts and
> decisions and actions: the light of life that glows
> from heart and face, yes, every cell of the body.
> —*Myrtle Fillmore's Healing Letters*

Realization leads to demonstration, or expression, or embodiment of the absolute principle in a relative circumstance. What you recognize and integrate, you can realize. This is an essential movement in affirmative prayer, realizing what you can be, what you can know, and what you can activate in your life.

REFLECT AND PRACTICE

⑨ Thinking about a particular concern, select one power or quality to name and claim. Write it down.

> *In the midst of _____, I know God is _____, and therefore I Am _____.*

⑨ Take some time in meditation, resting as the *I AM*. What do you notice about your "problems" from this consciousness? What is the experience of I AM-ness like for you?

⑨ What does it mean to you that you can realize—make real—your divine identity in a particular demonstration?

  ⑨ What has stood in the way of your making this claim?

  ⑨ What do you sense you need to give up/release/ negate in order to make this claim?

  ⑨ What difference might it make in your life and work to agree God is ... I AM ... I Can ...?

CHAPTER 7
The Affirmative Prayer Flow

We have devoted time in the previous chapters to the foundational principles that support affirmative prayer: *I open* to a new understanding, recognizing *God is*, integrating *I AM*, and realizing *I can*. Now that we have an understanding of how each movement leads to the next, let's look at the entire prayer flow in more depth.

This prayer flow arose organically from the historical Five-Step Affirmative Prayer Process in Unity. The classical process is:

1. Relaxation
2. Concentration
3. Meditation
4. Realization
5. Gratitude

Linda and DeeAnn explored what was actually happening in each of the classic steps. We identified what was happening during our most impactful prayers, and we then began to rename the process, making the intent clearer and more understandable to a contemporary audience. We designed the concept of a "prayer flow" to bring about a consciousness shift. It is structured as a pathway toward claiming spiritual power and realizing it in actionable ways.

The first thing we noticed, as stated earlier, was that the affirmative prayer process is not really a step-by-step, paint-by-numbers formula. It is more like a fern frond that unfurls as consciousness expands. Affirmative prayer is a progression of movements that flow toward a new awareness. The spiral opening outward and expanding is an apt symbol of what we now call the affirmative prayer flow.

We considered the probable intent and action of each of the prayer segments in the classic five steps. The first step, relaxation, implies a release of tension. While this segment traditionally centers on relaxing the body, we realized that the beginning of the prayer flow is an invitation to something deeper. We are invited to relax everything—the tension in our body, yes, but also the story we have been telling, what we have been carrying in our mind and in our heart. The first moments of affirmative prayer establish our readiness, openness, and willingness for a new possibility, a divine understanding. Our willingness to open to something new creates the space for a shift in consciousness. Effective affirmative prayer rests on the willingness to see ourselves and the world anew. The first movement in the prayer flow now starts with *I Open* to a new possibility.

The next step, concentration, is a call to concentrate on the Divine, on God, to consciously shift from the conditions and experience of the world to the realm of the absolute. What we found is that to concentrate on the Divine, we first needed to recognize and name what God is. Recognizing a specific divine principle or power is key to the movement in prayer toward spiritual realization. Our model's next movement is *I recognize God is ...*

Placing the meditation step in the middle of the classical five-step prayer process has long been one of its more confusing aspects. Was it a call to be still in the midst of the prayer? Was it about the consciousness of meditation itself? Meditation is the practice where we invite our sense of separation to dissolve and welcome an awareness of oneness. Our small awareness falls away and we claim the I AM. I AM consciousness is one of full integration—we are divine. Our nomenclature for the third movement, then, is *I Integrate I AM.*

Charles Fillmore defined realization as the dawning of Truth in consciousness. It is an "Aha!" moment of spiritual alignment when what we have recognized and integrated, we can now actualize. The action of realization is how we live into our divinity more fully, what we can actually do and have because of our divine identity. It is in realization that we activate a divine principle in time and space. Our model titles this movement *I realize I can, I have, I know.*

Gratitude is the final step in the classical steps of affirmative prayer. Typically, gratitude is given to God for getting what was asked for in the prayer. In affirmative prayer we are shifting consciousness, not petitioning for a specific outcome. The final movement of the prayer is actually appreciation for our shift in consciousness, appreciation for the new understanding, and appreciation that the prayer itself brought about a realization of Truth. Our model's final movement ends the prayer flow with *I appreciate* the shift in consciousness.

In summary, our model, arising from the historical model in Unity, contains five movements that make up the affirmative prayer flow:

> **I open** to new possibility
> **I recognize** God is
> **I integrate** I Am
> **I realize** I can, I have, I know
> **I appreciate** the shift in consciousness

Five Movements of Affirmative Prayer

	Action	Movements	Historical Steps
1	I open to a new possibility	Opening	Relaxation
2	God is ...	Recognition	Concentration
3	*I Am ...*	Integration	Meditation
4	I can, I have, I know	Realization	Realization
5	I appreciate the shift in consciousness	Appreciation	Gratitude

As we have shown, each movement leads to the next. As we inhabit each movement, our consciousness, like a fern frond, unfurls from the tension of a prayer concern toward the expansiveness of divine realization. It is in the realization that we can concretely activate the divinity we are.

In a moment we will take a closer look at each movement and the language we can use as we move through each movement. We will begin with personal prayer and in later chapters address how to pray affirmatively with others. Let's begin by looking at what moves us to step into prayer.

Condition and Purpose

Affirmative prayer is applicable to all of life's moments, the joys and sorrows. We can engage in affirmative prayer when we are grateful so that we can experience even more of what we are feeling gratitude for. While we can use affirmative prayer to bless the good in our lives, most of us will reach for affirmative prayer when life is challenging. When we are struggling to remember our divine identity, affirmative prayer can effectively realign us with our true nature. Therefore, the majority of prayer requests begin with some sort of challenge, condition, or circumstance. We do not attempt to control the condition with affirmative prayer. Instead, we open to a shift in our consciousness that transforms how we experience conditions and heal at the level of mind. As taught in New Thought, transformation is an inside job. Therefore, we begin with a condition.

> Condition: *My brother and I are not speaking, and I fear I have lost him forever.*

There are those in New Thought who hold to the idea that by articulating a condition, we are giving that condition more power and energy in our lives, so we shouldn't focus on what is challenging. They adhere to the practice of purposefully guarding every word or thought as if the smallest worry will lead to even worse situations. As touched upon earlier when discussing negations, pretending something isn't active in our life is not true healing. It is by meeting our worries, doubts, and fears with Truth that we heal. Pretending a condition doesn't exist is what we call a spiritual bypass. Do not be afraid to name what is happening within. The affirmative prayer process allows you to powerfully meet your loss, pain, fear, and doubt with Truth.

When praying affirmatively we are looking for a spiritual antidote to the condition. That is what we will ultimately place our attention upon—the spiritual antidote that will shift our consciousness. In this example: *My brother and I are not speaking, and I fear I have lost him forever,* we would be well reminded that we have no control over whether our brother will want to speak with us again. We cannot coerce or force him to do anything. What we can do is be open to a new understanding of Truth that alters our assumptions and intentions.

> The important need is not to try to effect some change in other people [or circumstances] but

to make some changes in your thoughts [and feelings] about them. Don't try to set them right, but rather to see them rightly. And to see them rightly you must get rid of some narrow frames of reference, and get out of the feeling of concern.
—Eric Butterworth, *The Universe Is Calling*

The purpose of affirmative prayer is to align with whatever divine principle will meet, heal, and transform a false sense of separation. We focus the purpose of the prayer on what we want to realize and experience.

Purpose: *To align myself with the harmonizing power of love and a deeper awareness of oneness with my brother.*

As we become clear and intentional in the prayer's purpose, we have already begun the process of transformation.

In other prayers, a single condition might yield several different purposes. The purpose of prayer is focused on what would be useful for you right now, and that can vary depending on what you need right now. For example:

Condition: *I feel tired and run-down. I have no energy.*

Purpose 1: *To align with the inexhaustible resources that I AM, welcoming zeal and enthusiasm.*

Purpose 2: *To align with wisdom and open to discerning what is truly mine to do.*

Purpose 3: *To align with strength and unlock hidden reservoirs of determination.*

Our purpose is what directs and focuses our prayer. The beautiful thing about affirmative prayer is you can always pray again. If a prayer that aligns you with zeal doesn't shift your understanding, you can always align with wisdom or strength the next time you pray.

Now that we have a purpose for our prayer, we are ready to move into the prayer flow itself. To be clear, the words that we use in the prayer flow arise from a state of consciousness. We are not speaking *about* opening, recognizing, integrating, realizing, and appreciating—we are speaking *from* an experience of them. The more we practice the prayer flow, the more aligned we become with this embodied experience.

Movement One: I Open

The first movement is making space. It is about opening our heart, our mind, our beingness to a new understanding. It is about being willing to shift and realign with divine principle. *I Open* is preparing a space in consciousness for something new to arise. It is consciously cultivating a state of willingness so we can remember the Truth of our divine identity. How we might articulate this first movement, our experience of opening, will be unique for each of us. Part of the power of affirmative prayer is just how personal it is. The examples listed below are just that, examples. They offer a glimpse of the possibilities for this movement. You are invited to sit with what *I Open* means to you. What language supports and activates your willingness for a new understanding?

> In this moment I quiet my mind, open my heart, and choose to allow myself the possibility of a new perspective, one that is grounded in spiritual principle and in my infinite potential. In this moment, I consciously open to what is possible.

> In this moment I pause and open my heart. I become still and allow for a new understanding.

In this moment I breathe, consciously placing my attention on something larger than what I currently know.

In this moment I come to a full stop and open my heart, my mind, and my being.

I relax my body and open my mind to the truth I am seeking. I open my heart to the glory of the light within me. I am in a state of expectancy, ready for my good.

I open to what I don't know but long to know, the deepest wisdom that I AM.

I am open-minded, openhearted. In the spirit of "let there be ..." I step into the power of it, calling myself to "let me be ..." Let me be open, curious, and expectant. Let me be open and ready to see more clearly the light I AM, the potential I have. I AM open. I breathe into the spaciousness of my open heart. I am ready. I am willing.

Notice that none of these examples include addressing an outer deity. For many, the long-established habit of starting prayer with "Dear God" or "Sweet Spirit" is hard to break. Such terminology reinforces separation consciousness, making it difficult for us to realize our divine identity. The potential in the opening statement of prayer is our consciousness opening to Truth rather than getting God's attention. Students often claim they understand oneness even when they say "Dear God." We invite you instead to say what you mean, to describe your personal experience of opening to a new possibility. As we continue to move through the prayer flow, notice the value of this distinction.

What if we can't get past our story and can't truly become willing to open? Prayer is happening within us, after all. If we aren't truly willing, then how can a prayer truly support a shift in our consciousness? When we are struggling to see possibility, negations are a powerful way to support a shift and opening. Here, we have taken two of the examples from above and incorporated negations. Notice how you can effectively pair affirmations and negations. Together they provide support for an authentic shift from a limited narrative to infinite possibility.

> *In this moment I quiet my mind, open my heart. I release what has come before and what is coming after. I center in this present moment and choose to allow myself the possibility of a new perspective, one that is grounded in spiritual principle and in my infinite potential. As I exhale, any resistance to this opening dissolves away effortlessly. As I inhale into this moment, I consciously let go of where I have been, and open to what is possible.*

> *I relax my body and open my mind to the truth I am seeking. I release any tension in my body, mind, and heart. I open my heart to the glory of the light within me. I consciously pivot my focus from the circumstances. I am in a state of expectancy, ready for my good.*

Negations and affirmations can be paired in any movement. Negations allow us to meet our humanness authentically and compassionately.

Now that we are open to a new understanding, we are ready to move into alignment with the purpose of our prayer.

Movement Two: Recognize *God Is*

As outlined in Chapter 4, in this movement we are recognizing and naming the divine principles that we are seeking to realign with and activate in our lives. *God is* recognizes what is useful to us right now. Specifically, any divine principle that seems to be lacking. If we are worried, then perhaps we want to know more peace. If afraid, then perhaps faith. If angry, then perhaps harmony. What we choose to recognize is what is most useful to us right now. When we recognize and focus on a divine principle, we magnify it in consciousness.

> *I recognize there is only one power and one presence and it is wisdom—the deep, innate, intuitive knowing that is present in seeds blooming or birds taking flight—and it is available right now.*

> *I recognize the love that is everywhere present, harmonizing and unifying all that there is—that love is available and accessible right now.*

> *I recognize the joy that is nearer than my breath, that is constant, unchanging, and ever-present and that is not dependent on circumstance.*

> *I recognize abundance, seeing it everywhere present—in the leaves of the trees and the grains of sand and the drops of water in the ocean.*

> *I recognize peace in this moment. Peace that passes all understanding. Peace that is available and accessible, that is unchanging and ever constant. Peace that is the very fabric of All That Is.*

And just as in *I Open*, if we are struggling to honestly recognize some aspect of the Divine, we can use negations to move past any limiting beliefs.

> *I recognize that there is only one power and one presence, and it is wisdom. I release any belief that wisdom could be lacking or not available in this moment. I recognize it in the deep, innate, intuitive*

knowing that is present in seeds blooming and in birds taking flight. Wisdom is available right now.

Now that we have recognized what is useful right now, it is time to integrate and claim that divine principle as our own.

Movement Three: Integrate *I AM*

In this movement, we can now claim the divine principle we chose. We identify with the principle. Integrating our divine identity, we stand in innate spiritual authority, in *I AM*.

> Remember that the object of all treatment (affirmative prayer) is to raise the mind to the Christ consciousness, through which all true healing is accomplished.
> —Charles Fillmore, *Teach Us to Pray*

I joyfully claim my divine identity. I am one with the universal presence and I am one with wisdom. Wisdom is mine to access and activate.

From the awareness of oneness, I integrate as my Christ self. Strength is mine. I am strength. I am determination. I am steadfastness.

As I recognize wholeness, I integrate and embrace my divine identity, which is wholeness. I AM wholeness!

The one life is abundance and I AM the one life. Abundance is my name and true nature.

As the I AM, I have named and now claim joy. Joy is my true nature.

Order is my divine identity. I claim the adjusting power of order.

Negations can once again be used to support integrating and claiming our I AM.

I joyfully claim my divine identity. Any sense of separation falls away and I say yes to Truth. I am one with the universal presence and I am one with wisdom. I release any sense of unworthiness. Wisdom is mine to access and activate.

Movement Four: *I Realize I Can, I Have, I Know*

We have opened a space for possibility, recognized a needed spiritual principle, integrated this divine principle with our own divine identity, and we are now ready to step into realization of what is possible. *Realizing I can, I have, I know* is where we move from a divine idea into an actualized reality. In New Thought, answered prayer is often called a demonstration, meaning a demonstration of divine principle manifesting in time and space. This unfolds through our realization of what is now possible: that we can, we have, or we know what is ours to do, to be, or to understand. It is where what we desire is made real through our embodiment of the principle. Myrtle Fillmore said it this way:

This is our method of prayer: acknowledging our oneness with God, claiming the ability that this gives, and expecting to have the things needed and conducive to spiritual progress.
—*Myrtle Fillmore's Healing Letters*

Notice that our definition of "answered prayer" is not a magical result or a supreme being granting our wish. Answered

95

prayer is when we are changed because of our spiritual realization, which leads to a transformed experience.

What we could not see, understand, or know when we were caught in our human perspective has now shifted as we align with our spiritual nature. We can now see, know, and understand from this larger awareness. As we practice this process we can trust and expect this shift in consciousness. We can expect a realignment. We can expect an "Aha!" moment where we now can embody and live from our divine nature.

> *From this I AM consciousness, where wisdom is mine to access, I know that I can discern what is mine to do. I know that my intuition is aligned with my highest purpose, and I can trust and rely on that intuitive awareness. I can relax and trust that I am choosing wisely. I have all that I need to move through these choices with ease, grace, and flow.*

> *Embracing strength as my true nature and true name, I bring purpose and determination to this project. I have the fortitude and steadfastness to navigate the schedule shifts and any other perceived obstacles to finishing on time. I am strong, steadfast, and determined as I proceed.*

Notice how the realization movement of the prayer is actionable. It is how we can actualize, demonstrate, and embody that principle in time and space. It can be challenging to grasp realization without seeing how recognition and integration lead us to this new awareness.

Let's take a look at some examples of how *God is* and *I AM* lead to a new realization of what I can, I have, I know. Each of these examples begins with a condition and focuses on the three movements at the heart of affirmative prayer: recognition, integration, and realization.

I'm worried about my loved one who's been hospitalized in intensive care.

God Is

I recognize God is life, the principle of life, the irrepressible flow, vitality, and vigor evident within each life form.

I AM

I AM the principle of life. I claim that I AM and my loved one is the very flow of life, the vitality of life that is evident in her presence.

I Can, I Have, I Know

I can focus my mind on my loved one's life, the fullness of life that is evident right now in all the functions of her body that are doing their part for her recovery.

I have the capacity to focus on her wholeness, the whole of her life, rather than obsess over what appears wrong.

I speak to her of all that she loves about life, knowing and emphasizing her wholeness.

Here is another example:

I lost my job and don't know how I'm going to pay my bills.

God Is

I recognize God is strength—stability, courage, and tenacity.

I AM

I AM one with and now claim the principle of strength. I stand steady and stable in the midst of shifting emotions and day-to-day conditions. I am courageous. I am tenacious, persistent, and enduring.

I Can, I Have, I Know

I can keep my thoughts focused on the possibilities ahead, steadfast in knowing the truth of abundance.

I have the courage to pursue the job of my dreams, working diligently for my greatest good.

I know that I can persist through daily ups and downs without having a setback set me back, tenaciously envisioning and following my highest intentions for my next employment.

And a third example:

I want to improve my relationship with my significant other/parent/child/friend.

God Is

I recognize God is the principle of love—harmonizing and unifying.

I AM

I AM and now claim the principle of love. I AM the embodiment of love. I and my loved one are love and have the business of love at hand between us.

I Can, I Have, I Know

I can harmonize my thoughts about our relationship.

I know above all that I am one with my beloved—I see myself in my beloved.

I know and live into the truth that we are integrally, eternally one in love.

I have the capacity to do my part to send nonverbal as well as verbal messages that I am willing to remain connected in our shared experience.

Negations in this movement might look like this:

I can release any thoughts of enmity and harmonize my thoughts about our relationship.

I release any idea that my beloved and I are separate. I know above all that I am one with my beloved—I see myself in my beloved.

I let go of my human understanding of love based on conditions. I know and live into the truth that we are integrally, eternally one in love.

I let go of any streams of thought contributing to resentment. I have the capacity to do my part to send nonverbal as well as verbal messages that I am willing to remain connected in our shared experience.

I Appreciate

As we step into the final movement of the prayer flow, let us start by explaining the switch from the word *gratitude* in the classic five steps to *appreciation*. Both are synonyms and interchangeable. However, the two words are subtly distinctive. Gratitude is a feeling generally expressed outwardly for perceived blessings and is given to another person or group of people. Although gratitude reveals what we appreciate or value, closing a prayer with statements of appreciation acknowledges the value of our realization.

Particularly, to conclude prayer with appreciation for a particular spiritual realization reinforces our consciousness shift. It retains our realization of oneness or nonduality. It amplifies or increases in value the truth we have identified.

Appreciation is more than a turn of phrase, more than a crafted statement. It is a state of being itself, evident in biochemistry and invisible vibration. Appreciation is a natural result of expanded awareness, and it is unrelated to human conditions.

The entire prayer comes together in this final movement as we express appreciation for a realization of Truth. We are appreciating the shift in our own consciousness, the new understanding we just realized and how we can incorporate it going forward. We are not thanking an outside deity. We are not grateful for a manifestation that will come at some point down the road. We are appreciating the shift that has happened within us right now. Affirmative prayer is always happening in the present moment. We appreciate that all we have desired is fulfilled in the present moment and we are now transformed.

> *I appreciate this new understanding, all I have realized, and all that I now know myself capable of being.*

I appreciate seeing the truth of this situation and knowing how to show up as the I AM, as wisdom and love.

I appreciate all that has been revealed and the growth and expansion of my spiritual understanding.

I appreciate my capacity to realign and anchor Truth and to be that Truth in all my interactions.

I celebrate my Godness, my true nature. To know the Truth I am now aware of, to live in the spirit of this newfound freedom, I rejoice!

In totality, these five movements guide us unerringly to a new awareness of our true nature and provide a road map to actualizing our divine nature in time and space. Again, here are the five movements of the affirmative prayer flow:

1. **I open.** Breathing deeply, relaxing my body, and focusing within, I create space for a new understanding.

2. **I recognize** *God is.* I recognize there is only one power and presence, and I can describe it as life, love, wisdom, or any divine principle that appears needed.

3. **I integrate** *I AM.* I am fully human and fully divine. I begin to see the power of God is the very power within me. I declare I AM that very power.

4. **I realize.** Therefore, I conclude that I have within me the power to be, to do, to have, to allow, and to

experience wholeness in new, specific, actionable ways.

5. **I appreciate.** Grateful for my growing spiritual awareness and the fulfillment of prayer that has already happened, I am empowered to live fully now and into a fulfilling future.

Here are a few examples of complete prayer flows. The first uses the condition and purpose we started with earlier in the chapter. The second provides the complete prayer flow of an earlier example that only focused on the heart of affirmative prayer.

Condition: My brother and I are not speaking, and I fear I have lost him forever.

Purpose: To align myself with the harmonizing power of love and a deeper awareness of oneness with my brother.

I Open
I open to the awareness that there is a new under-standing about my brother available to me. I breathe and open to this possibility. I am willing to see anew.

God Is
I recognize there is only one power and one pres-ence active in the universe. It is love. It is compas-sion. Love is everywhere present, always available and accessible.

I AM
I know that I AM one within the One. The one power that is perfect love, that is infinite compassion, is

what I AM. It is the Truth about my brother as well. I AM the living expression of love and compassion.

I Can, I Have, I Know
Therefore, as love, I can see love and be love. In the state of love, resentments naturally fall away and compassion rules my understanding. I see my brother as his divine self and I love him. I see myself as my divine self and know I am loved. Our connection is clear—a living expression of love and compassion. I am this and I see myself as this when I am with him. I say yes to anchoring love; it will guide how I speak and what I say. I allow compassion to be my true north in all our interactions. There are no obstacles to love.

I Appreciate
How grateful I am for this deeper awareness of who I am, of who he is. I appreciate and give thanks for love as my identity and his identity. We are forever one in love. And so it. Amen.

Condition: I lost my job and don't know how I'm going to pay my bills.

Purpose: I pursue my next job from a position of inner strength and prosperity consciousness.

I Open
I now breathe deeply and slowly, quieting my mind and opening my heart, ready for a fresh perspective of Truth that I need.

God Is
I recognize God is strength—stability, courage, and tenacity.

I Am
I am and I now claim the principle of strength. I stand steady and stable in the midst of shifting emotions and day-to-day conditions. I am courageous, able to think and act in my own best interests. I am tenacious, persistent, and enduring.

I Can, I Have, I Know
I can keep my thoughts focused on the possibilities ahead, steadfast in knowing the truth of abundance.

I have the courage to pursue the job of my dreams.

I know I can persist through daily ups and downs without having a setback set me back, tenaciously envisioning and following my highest intentions for my next employment.

I Appreciate
Thankful for spiritual insight and a fresh perspective based in Truth, I proceed in joyful anticipation.

Here is an example of how the prayer movements effortlessly flow together:

With every breath, strong and intentional, I clear my mind and open my heart, becoming fully present in this moment. I recognize only one power, the power of God that is the fullness of life. Divine life is whole and intact. It cannot be diminished or threatened by any human condition. Divine life is my life. I am the power of divine life; therefore, I vibrate with wholeness and well-being. Now and in the moments ahead, I celebrate as I choose the fullness of life.

REFLECT AND PRACTICE

⑨ How do you understand gratitude and appreciation? Is there a difference for you?

⑨ Close your eyes for a moment and bring something or someone to mind that you appreciate and/or are grateful for. What do you notice happens when you spend time focusing this way?

⑨ Referring to "Affirming the 12 Powers as Principles" from the Unity Prayer Ministry (at the end of this chapter), select three powers and apply them to appropriate conditions and use them in the prayer process.

⑨ Here are some conditions for which people commonly seek prayer support. Choose a spiritual principle/power that could be an antidote for each of these conditions. Select two or three and write an affirmative prayer, following the Affirmative Prayer Flow Template (at the end of this chapter), as if you were experiencing these conditions.

   ⑨ Divorce/breakup

   ⑨ Unemployment

   ⑨ Diagnosis of a disease

- ◎ Argument with family member

- ◎ Exam/test

- ◎ Upcoming travel

- ◎ Looking for a new home

- ◎ Losing weight

- ◎ Loved one enters hospice care

◎ Each day this week, write your personal prayers following the template. What do you notice at the close of the week about your prayer consciousness and developing skill?

Affirming the 12 Powers as Principles

Each of the 12 powers can be recognized and integrated in prayer. Use this as a reference for learning some of the aspects of the powers and how they may be applied specifically for prayer concerns. For example, if you are following the flow of prayer and focusing on the heart of affirmative prayer—God is, I AM, I can—then an example of prayer about discord in a relationship might be:

I recognize God is: God is the source of faith, the perceiving power.

I integrate I AM: That means that I AM the perceiving power of faith.

I realize I can: Knowing this, I can look beyond appearances to find Truth in my relationship, and to perceive what I might contribute toward peace between us.

Or:

I recognize God is the source of conviction (faith).

I integrate I AM the power of conviction, the ability to know without question before any improvement manifests.

I realize I can trust what has not yet appeared, confident in our capacity for a healthy relationship.

Or another example from a different power:

I recognize God is order, the adjusting power.

I integrate I AM the power of adjustment, the ability to change direction and respond well as the need arises.

I realize I can reorder my thinking about this relationship, remaining open to renegotiating our agreements and being responsive to new ideas.

Below you will find descriptions of each power and how they can be used.

Faith

The perceiving power of faith; look beyond appearances to find Truth.

The conviction of faith; trust what has not yet appeared.

The expectancy of faith; prepare for fulfillment of my heart's desires.

Imagination

The conceiving power of imagination; catch hold of divine ideas.

The visioning power of imagination; shape a mental image of my desired reality.

The power of embodiment (imagination); behave in concert with my desired reality.

Understanding

> The power of comprehension (understanding); make sense of my experience.
>
> The power of realization (understanding); realize my divine identity.
>
> The power of insight (understanding); learn from my life.

Will

> The power of choice (will); say *yes* to the one thing that is most important to me.
>
> The power of commitment (will); fulfill a promise to myself to follow through on what I have chosen.
>
> The power of willingness (will); recommit any time I have failed to fulfill my promise to myself.

Zeal

> The power of enthusiasm (zeal); celebrate moments every day.
>
> The power of audacity (zeal); take bold action even when unpopular.
>
> The power of devotion (zeal); devote my time and energy to my purpose.

Power

> The power of concentration (power); focus my attention on what is most important.
>
> The power of self-mastery (power); discipline my thoughts and guard my reactions; know when to speak up and when to remain quiet; respond rather than react.
>
> The power of spiritual authority (power); tell the Truth to myself and others.

Love

The magnetizing power of love; follow my heart's desires.

The harmonizing power of love; harmonize my thoughts, words, and actions.

The power of unity (love); behold the Divine in myself and others.

Wisdom

The power of right judgment (wisdom); evaluate options and make sound choices.

The power of discernment (wisdom); listen underneath logic for inspiration.

The power of intuition (wisdom); trust and follow my inner sense of direction.

Strength

The stabilizing power of strength; stand steady in Truth during changing circumstances.

The power of courage (strength); be courageous, take healthy risks, and advocate for myself and others.

The power of tenacity (strength); stay the course; keep going forward; persist.

Order

The power of organization (order); put my thoughts and actions in order; move from thought to action in an orderly flow.

The adjusting power of order; change my actions when the circumstances change; shift my focus when necessary.

The evolutionary power of order; learn from my experience; grow in knowledge and awareness day by day.

Release/Negation

The cleansing power of negation (or release or elimination); softly acknowledge when I have been thinking in terms that are limited or false.

The power of renunciation; say an emphatic *no!* when I recognize I have been holding a false belief.

The power of repentance; turn around, start again, saying *no* to the false and *yes* to the truth.

Life

The animating power of life; flow in continuous renewal and forward-moving progress.

The power of vitality (life); give life to my dreams and intentions.

The power of presence (life); shine the light in every circumstance; be a compassionate presence; share the gift of my spiritual awareness.

Affirmative Prayer Flow Template

A. State the condition that you are experiencing and want to change.
B. State the purpose of the prayer by identifying the desired state of mind and/or principle to claim.

Condition: _____

Purpose: _____

1. I Open

I open and create space for a new understanding, relaxing into what is possible.

_____

_____

2. I Recognize: God Is

There is only one power and one presence. I recognize and name the divine ideas/principles that would be useful, specifically those principles that seem to be lacking.

_____

_____

3. I Integrate: I AM

Awareness of the I AM, integrating human and divine identity, claiming the divine principles and qualities just recognized.

_____

_____

4. I Realize: I Can, I Have, I Know

Realizing what my divinity makes possible. Affirming, activating, claiming, realizing those divine ideas by which I can experience wholeness in new, specific, and actionable ways.

_____

_____

5. I Appreciate

Appreciation for how consciousness has been changed/aligned and that the prayer is fulfilled/done right now—not in the future.

_____

_____

CHAPTER 8
When Prayer Seems Not to Be Working

We now understand the core spiritual principles that are at work in affirmative prayer. We are practicing and using the affirmative prayer flow. We are opening to a shift in consciousness. We may even be realizing that shift in our prayer work. And yet, what is going on when our prayers don't seem to be working? When our prayers aren't "answered"? Or, in classic New Thought terminology, aren't "demonstrating"? What is happening or not happening when our prayers don't seem to work? Here are some possibilities.

Outlining

Outlining is where we are being so specific about our desire, we have outlined it so particularly, that there is no room for us to see any other possibility. We are incapable of seeing beyond our limited view.

A perfect illustration of outlining occurs in the classic joke about the man on his roof in a flood praying for God to save him from the rising waters. As the man prays for a miracle, a neighbor pulls up in his car and invites the man to join him. The man says, "No thanks, I'm waiting on a miracle from God." The waters continue to rise and a boat comes by but the man says, "No thanks, I'm waiting on a miracle from God." Next a helicopter appears and the man again says, "No thanks, I'm waiting on a miracle from God." As the flood waters continue to rise and ultimately sweep him away to his death, he finds himself at the pearly gates and there is God. The man says, "God! I was waiting on you for a miracle!" And God says, "I sent you a car, a boat, and a helicopter—what more did you want?"

When we are so fixated on what we think is supposed to happen, we miss what is available to us right now. We miss opportunities because we have limited ourselves and what is possible to a very narrow focus.

Affirmative prayer is not praying *for* something—it is awakening *to* something. It is about a shift in consciousness. As we live from this new understanding, our world changes. If our prayer is "not working," or if our experience is unchanged after prayer, it may be helpful to reflect on whether we are limiting or outlining. Are we fixated on a specific outcome that is blinding us to what else is possible? Are we so attached to a single desired outcome that we have closed our mind to other, possibly greater, demonstrations?

Influence of Collective Consciousness

Our thoughts and beliefs are creative. And while it is true that we have the spiritual authority to create our experience, it is also incomplete without factoring in the collective consciousness.

In addition to our personal thoughts and beliefs, collective thoughts and beliefs also shape and impact our experience. Collective beliefs, also known as *race consciousness* in classic New Thought (meaning human race consciousness), are always evolving and growing. Five hundred years ago everyone believed the sun circled around the earth. Even after Copernicus put forth the heliocentric model in the mid-1500s, it took another 100 years for that information to begin to be accepted in scientific circles. Galileo, who saw the truth of this model through his telescope, was condemned as a heretic. It wasn't until the early 1800s that the Catholic Church accepted the heliocentric model.

New ideas and understandings take time to become part of human consciousness. That evolutionary process has been speeding up. A century ago humanity didn't have aviation, space travel, instantaneous communications, or video conferences. We now accept those as the norm. Collectively, we are evolving faster than ever before.

While the evolution of consciousness may be speeding up, it still does take time. Even if we are doing our best to expand our understanding of principle, for instance the principle of prosperity, the collective belief that denies that new understanding of prosperity will impact us.

The stock market is a perfect illustration of collective consciousness in action. It is ultimately not connected to anything but the confidence of its investors. When the collective consciousness of investors is confident, the market rises; when it isn't, the market falls. That is why the economy itself can be struggling while the market is strong.

In modern vernacular, we can also understand collective consciousness as "group think." We accept certain beliefs and understandings because everyone around us believes them. Collective consciousness beliefs, just like individual beliefs, can be overt or hidden.

Our individual and collective beliefs are like the operating system of a computer. Some programming we can see and know how to use. Some is embedded so deeply we don't see it working. If we are not experiencing a consciousness shift, or if we are not demonstrating after our prayers, we can reflect on whether collective beliefs might be impacting us. What hidden beliefs do we have that align with the limited collective consciousness?

Years ago, Linda struggled financially. Paying bills every payday felt defeating, as less money was flowing in than flowing out for the needs of her family. She would set aside a little each pay period in case of an unexpected, large expense, which invariably came. It seemed she would never get ahead and build wealth. Studying New Thought prosperity teachings, Linda began to notice she had been operating from a chorus of false beliefs in collective consciousness, buried but active. She had heard again and again in childhood: *Money doesn't grow on trees; we can't afford it;* and *there's never enough.* Consciously considering these adages in light of prosperity teachings, Linda was able to challenge and correct her unconscious hold on beliefs that had been given to her.

The process of making our hidden and collective beliefs visible is a powerful part of how we grow collectively and individually. Collective consciousness, by its very nature, identifies what a majority of people currently understand. As we uplevel our personal consciousness, we also uplevel the collective consciousness. As we continue to evolve personally, so too does the collective consciousness evolve. This is the powerful process of evolution and expansion, and it begins within each of us.

To explain further, social injustice issues are all based in collective consciousness. People in marginalized populations who experience injustice did not create their circumstances. Similarly, people experiencing cancer did not create cancer. Cancer is currently a collective consciousness condition just as smallpox was in an earlier era. Nevertheless, individuals can heal from the harm done by the collective consciousness and contribute to human evolution in the process.

Affirmative prayer is an impactful, powerful tool for this great work. It provides us with a process for transformation and facilitates a shift in our experience. Experience is real-time feedback as to whether we have actualized transformation or not. If our life experience hasn't shifted, then there is something more to shift in our awareness. Affirmative prayer is a process of transformation that facilitates the evolution of consciousness. We recommend including the tool of negation and affirmation (Chapter 4), which is designed to bring subconscious beliefs to the surface.

Being aware of the impact of collective consciousness, we can be gentle with ourselves and others. If the spiritual work we are doing feels challenging, or bigger than us, we can acknowledge that it *is* bigger than us. This is what makes our work so powerful: When *we* shift, we influence collective consciousness. The invitation is to be kind and supportive to ourselves as we engage in this great work. Rather than condemn ourselves, we can release any shame or guilt stemming from a belief that we have caused any challenges we are experiencing in our life. We can practice compassion for ourselves and the world and be a willing space for possibility. Our healing helps heal the collective consciousness, making a world that works for everyone.

The Energy Hump

Remember Mind-Idea-Expression? The creative process includes a natural energy hump that shows up when we are moving from divine principles into material form. This can also be called "trouble at the border." We commonly resist manifestation as we move from thought (formless state) to actualization in time and space (form).

An energy hump is actually a gift. Imagine what life would be like if everything we thought, believed, or desired demonstrated immediately? The energy hump is a slowing down, a concretizing of something into form. It is an invitation to explore what we need to become. Breathing into the process, reflecting on how we can be our own answered prayer can shift abstract ideas into concrete, authentic action.

Another shape that an energy hump can take is resistance to manifestation attributable to an embedded theology of human insufficiency, such as "only God can change this situation" or "I'm only human." It can look like vagueness or lack of specificity, which is often merely unwillingness to identify some possible action we can take to demonstrate the principle we have recognized in prayer.

Lack of Specificity

Just as too much specificity can impact the power of our prayers, so can too little. Generalizing can result in a temporary sense of peace and well-being that is comforting but fleeting. When we have an awareness of a divine principle but don't activate that principle in time and space in some real, concrete way, it remains just an idea. There has to be enough specificity to move it through the energy hump. There also has to be enough room for a larger understanding to emerge.

The realization movement in affirmative prayer is where we move from an idea to concrete expression in time and space. Let's look at the following examples from the realization movement of an affirmative prayer.

> Example 1: *I am love and so all my relationships are loving.*
>
> Example 2: *I am love and I speak as love, and Tommy and I stop fighting.*
>
> Example 3: *I am love and I speak as love, actively look for love, and act from love in all my relationships. I know that love is present between Tommy and me no matter how angry we both may seem.*

Example 1 is true, lovely, and very general. It is an idea, unable to be activated in time and space.

Example 2 is actionable but it is also directive. Prayer is meant to shift our consciousness. As we shift our consciousness the fighting may stop, but limiting the prayer to one specific outcome does not leave room for Tommy to have his own experience, in his own time and in his own way. It makes the prayer dependent on Tommy's showing up in a certain way—our way.

Example 3 is actionable, something we can manifest in time and space. It is specific and yet not constricting. It leaves room for whatever may happen in time and space and anchors that there is something more important happening than the argument. It invites us into a new understanding, and it can only happen through us. This is how we can transform and shift our experiences.

The space between outlining and being too general is like *Goldilocks and the Three Bears*. It is through experimentation that we find the balance that is just right. In our prayer life we can experiment by zooming in with clear specificity and also zooming out for a broader perspective. Notice what arises, which is more familiar and comfortable, and which leads you to inspired action that demonstrates the principle you have recognized in prayer.

Magical Thinking

Magical thinking is like Example 2 above *(Tommy and I stop fighting)*. We might miss that we are the ones invited to change, expecting instead that the world should change to suit us and our needs. Magical thinking avoids growth and transformation. It wants to take the easy path. It can show up when our expectations are not aligned with our most authentic self. Just because we may pray to sing like Beyoncé does not mean that we will ever sing like Beyoncé. That desire is not connected to who we truly are; it is connected to our idea about talent or success or fame that is merely a construct unrelated to our own potential. We want to be our most authentic self, singing. Only Beyoncé can truly sing like Beyoncé. Each of us will sing in our own way. Each of us will develop our own talents and succeed as we realize our divine identity and develop healthy self-awareness.

No matter how hard we may practice or study or apply ourselves, sometimes the thing we think we want eludes us. Sometimes we feel frustrated by pressing forward despite a growing pull away from one thing and toward something else. As we continually change and grow, we are invited to embrace the process of our unfolding and evolution, knowing that everything is supporting our greatest good. Nothing is wasted. Nothing is lost.

DeeAnn's story illustrates how we, with the best of intentions, can create our own suffering even as we are evolving toward our greatest good.

DeeAnn was an actor for decades and loved it. She worked steadily, though it never quite took off in a way that was stable and solid. She was feeling frustrated, sad, and deeply disappointed as her dreams were stymied. She knew it was time for a change, but it was so hard to let go of the dream. It was deeply and profoundly painful not to realize fulfillment of the dream. She meditated and prayed on this every day, and one day saw a vision of herself wearing clerical robes. At that moment, she was so limited in what she thought was possible, so fixated on being an actor, that she saw her vision as proof she would land a role and play a minister on TV. Being a successful actor was the only framework she focused on and could not imagine anything beyond it.

She eventually came to see that she was afraid of losing her identity as an artist, creator, voice of possibility, and storyteller. Each shift in our consciousness can feel like a death because we are dying to who we thought we were. But each shift in our consciousness is also a rebirth as we live into who we truly are.

DeeAnn consciously opened, limiting less. She began to realize she was holding onto something that was about her ego, not her divine identity. Her call to ministry emerged like a beacon once she made space for it. She was ordained a minister—not playing one on TV—seven years later.

When we resist transformation, we create our own suffering. Our prayers not "working" can often mean we are afraid of the unknown, afraid of letting go, or afraid that we are losing something. We outline, we get caught in magical thinking, we get frustrated because we are having trouble at the border. All of this is an invitation to use the affirmative prayer flow. Bring your fear. Bring your frustration. Bring it all again and again. Allow realization of your divinity to emerge and transform your small ideas about who you have come here to be.

Uncovering and Transforming Hidden Beliefs

We have all experienced those moments when, regardless of how deeply or fiercely we pray, our experience does not shift, what we desire does not manifest. In those moments we are invited to deepen and explore what possible blocks we might have within ourselves. How are we invited to grow and transform?

Integrative affirmative prayer, or what Ernest Holmes called "argumentative prayer," is a powerful tool for uncovering hidden beliefs that do not serve us. It utilizes affirmation, negation, and inner dialogue to support an awakening to what we truly believe so that we can heal, transform, and elevate our limiting beliefs.

Integrative Affirmative Prayer Process

This ability to meet ourselves—to be present with our fears, worries, and doubts and meet them with Truth—is the heart of integrative affirmative prayer. It is a personal process for healing where we actively choose to listen for those voices of doubt, worry, or fear—not to squash them but to transform them.

The process begins by being willing to listen for an inner voice or feeling that does not align with Truth, no matter how "unspiritual" it may feel. In the midst of our personal use of the affirmative prayer flow, at any point that we are claiming and affirming Truth, we practice a deep listening to what is actually alive within us. For example, if we say:

I know that I am whole and perfect, and my body temple reflects this Truth.

What we might really be thinking and feeling is this:

But I broke my back. My body temple does not really reflect wholeness and perfection, and it never will.

This example is based on DeeAnn's real-life application of this process around a personal health challenge. If DeeAnn had chosen to ignore these doubts, then she would have been choosing a spiritual bypass. This teaching is not about pretending. It is not about saying something on the surface level while deep down we really believe something else. It is about aligning our deepest understanding of self with Truth to the best of our ability.

That voice of doubt was active in DeeAnn's consciousness and therefore it was active in her life. That doubt was also showing her exactly where she was invited to heal. It was an inner signal as to where to place her attention. Awareness of our false beliefs is the first step to freedom.

In the following example we will look at the realization movement of DeeAnn's prayer for healing. The italicized words are her doubts and fears. The unitalicized words are the prayer itself:

I know that I am whole and perfect, and my body temple reflects this Truth.

But I broke my back. My body temple does not really reflect wholeness and perfection, and it never will.

Rather than ignore that inner voice, we can purposefully shift our condition and purpose from where we started the prayer and instead navigate what is actually arising. The next part of the prayer will consciously and directly meet those beliefs with affirmations and negations anchored in spiritual principle.

> I know that possibility is always available. Any old beliefs, those old ideas that this body is not whole and perfect, that it can't be whole and perfect, I illuminate with the light of Truth. I hold them in love and I allow Truth to dissolve these false beliefs into the nothingness from which they came. They are not Truth. They have no power in my life. There is only one power and it is love, it is light, it is wholeness.

> *It would take a miracle for me to be fully healed.*

DeeAnn's inner doubt now shifts its argument in another direction and once again, our condition and purpose shifts to meet it with spiritual principle.

> I know the Divine expresses in ways that seem like miracles—in ways that seem impossible only because I have forgotten how powerful I am. I am powerful. I know that wholeness is always seeking to express as my life and I allow it—right now. I say *yes* to the miracle!

> *Is a miracle really possible?*

And we continue to meet any voice of doubt with more spiritual truth.

Anything and everything is possible in the infinite field of divine mind! I choose what is possible right now. My body temple is the perfect outpicturing of the divine idea of wholeness. There is only this Truth. There are no opposites to spiritual truth, so I now declare that all of my old beliefs that no longer serve me have no power over me. They have no authority. They are nothing, no thing. I am whole. I am perfect. I am healed. I am the miracle.

I am the miracle. I am the miracle. Yes, I AM the miracle!

By listening to the beliefs that are not in alignment with Truth, such as "It would take a miracle to be fully healed" or "Is a miracle really possible?" an incredibly potent and powerful personal affirmation arises: *I am the miracle*—an affirmation that is unique and that spoke and resonated with DeeAnn personally. While *I am whole and perfect* and *I say yes to the miracle!* are powerful affirmations, they were not meeting DeeAnn's deep-seated, limiting belief about powerlessness. *I AM the miracle!* met that need and shifted her consciousness in a new way.

The perception of wholeness is the consciousness of healing ... in practice ... the one who has the greatest feeling of wholeness and the greatest subjective embodiment of this wholeness will speak from the greatest degree of wholeness.
—Ernest Holmes, *Seminar Lectures*
(Los Angeles Science of Mind Communications)

And we would add: They will then concretely *experience* a greater degree of wholeness as their life.

Within our doubts and fears are the seeds of our healing. This is how we can transform our limited ideas. Not by avoiding them but by meeting them head-on with Truth.

Take some time to deeply listen to how you honestly respond to statements of Truth. Rather than gloss over them, invite them in. If you need to argue with those false beliefs, by all means do so. Argue with them until the arguments fall away. Which they will, for there is nothing more powerful than Truth. Your being wants to express as more wholeness, as you. We are wired to align with our divine nature. There is no argument that can arise within you that cannot be met with Truth.

REFLECT AND PRACTICE

- ◎ Where in your own life have you noticed magical thinking?

- ◎ When have you experienced an energy hump?

- ◎ Describe how the collective consciousness can work for you. Where have you felt the impact of collective consciousness in your own life?

- ◎ In your current prayer life, do you practice outlining (too much specificity) or the reverse, a lack of specificity? As you contemplate the Goldilocks "just right," what new understanding are you invited to explore?

- ◎ Practice using the integrative affirmative prayer process from this chapter to uncover hidden beliefs. Reflect on its value in shifting consciousness.

CHAPTER 9
Preparing to Pray with Others

The previous chapters provided building blocks to a powerful prayer process that supports personal healing and transformation. A natural extension of this practice is to share the prayer flow by praying with others. What does praying with others do to the prayer process and the ways we engage with it?

As has been discussed in previous chapters, affirmative prayer is not something we are doing to someone or something else. Affirmative prayer facilitates an alignment with our true nature that is unfurling within our own consciousness. We have no control over anyone else. We are inviting our own consciousness shift.

This premise is also the foundation of how we pray with others. Our focus is to move through the prayer flow and realize Truth. In our personal prayer life, this is a Truth about our own divinity. When praying with others, we are realizing the Truth about *their* divinity. It is by our spiritual authority to name and claim our own divine nature that we can also name and claim *their* divine nature.

In Unity, we specifically pray *with* people, not for people. We do not have access to something they don't have. Affirmatively praying with others is not about fixing their problem, convincing or coercing them to believe something, or even trying to make them feel better. It is affirming and realizing *within our own consciousness* that they already have access to everything and anything they need. We are anchoring the spiritual context through which their experience can be transformed. We are sharing our consciousness of oneness.

To illustrate what is meant by sharing our consciousness with others, think of our consciousness as a tuning fork. Through our personal prayer practice we have honed that tuning fork to vibrate at the frequency of our divinity. When we pray with others, our high vibration invites their consciousness to vibrate at that frequency along with us. We can also imagine our consciousness as a flame. Through our personal prayer practice our flame burns brightly and can ignite the flame in others to burn brightly as well.

If you remember DeeAnn's story from the introduction, the power of her experience in asking for prayer came not from someone meeting her in her despair. The healing and transformative power of that prayer arose precisely because the person praying with her saw only DeeAnn's divinity, not her brokenness. That person did not try to fix DeeAnn. That person did not tell DeeAnn what she should be feeling or believing. That person spoke declaratively about what they believed and knew. That person saw through human experience and named and claimed what they saw beyond the story so powerfully and clearly that DeeAnn's tuning fork shifted its frequency and her flame sputtered to life in a new way.

What does all this mean practically? It means that when you pray with others you are holding the high watch, anchoring spiritual truth, and not falling into their story. It means you are speaking from what you know. You cannot speak for what *they* know. Often when praying with others, to create a sense of connection and to affirm oneness, we will speak from the "we." Our intention is to include the person we are praying with, yet "we" can have the exact opposite result.

No "We-ing"

Affirmative prayer is happening within our own consciousness. We are speaking from our own divine understanding—from our I AM. We cannot speak to where anyone else is with any true authority. We may think we know where someone is in consciousness, but we cannot actually know. When we pray from our own understanding, we free the person we are praying with from thinking they have to feel or believe what we believe. As we speak from the "I," we allow them to have their own interior experience of transformation, one that is not dictated or decided by us. We allow them autonomy and do not presume to co-opt their consciousness.

Let's look at an example from the *I Open* movement of a prayer flow to highlight the subtle yet radical difference that is possible when we don't use "we" in our affirmative prayers. Here is an example of an opening movement that uses "we."

> *We take this moment to open our hearts and minds. We breathe as we shift our attention to what is possible.*

It is a lovely opening. We have taken our personal prayer process and expanded it to be a larger container. Instead of "I take this moment," the prayer moved to "we take this moment." Yet there are many assumptions happening within this simple shift in the opening movement. Let's take a closer look.

> *We take this moment to open our hearts and minds.*

When someone has come to us for prayer, we would certainly hope they can open their heart and mind. And yet they

128

have come for prayer precisely because they are struggling to do just that. Saying that "in this moment" they are supposed to be able to do something, when in reality they may not be there yet, creates an inner dissonance that undermines the purpose of affirmative prayer. We have no way of knowing whether they have opened their heart and mind. And while this may be difficult for those of us with compassionate hearts to hear, it is also none of our business.

Our ability to claim, name, and stand in spiritual authority is a hallmark of Unity and New Thought. Each of us has all that we need, and we are each striving personally to realize our divine nature. We cannot make someone understand their true nature. Whether their hearts are open or not, our only business in prayer—whether it is our personal prayer or when we pray with others—is whether our own heart is open.

We can see how the next sentence in our example continues to dictate and decide what this person's experience should be.

We breathe as we shift our attention to what is possible.

The truth is they very well may not be able to shift their attention just yet. Sometimes the pain is too much, the story too entrenched, and while the willingness may be present, we are not the ones in charge of the timing of the shift in their attention or in their consciousness.

By directing people to do something, even something as lovely as opening our hearts or taking a deep breath, we are telling them what they should be doing, what they should be feeling. Affirmative prayer is about creating a space where our consciousness shares the realization of our divinity. It is not telling, directing, or instructing someone how they should be feeling, being, and so on.

Let's look at an alternative that is spoken from the only awareness we can be sure of, our own.

The invitation in this moment is to open our hearts and minds. I breathe and I invite a shifting of attention to the possibility of a new understanding.

Notice how this example spoken from the "I" does not tell someone they have to be open or that they have to shift their attention. It is an invitation that illuminates what I am inviting to happen within my own consciousness. If they wish to join me, they can. Their autonomy and ability to choose is still their own. We do not want to *tell* people they are divine. We want them to be able to ignite their own divine awareness and know this for themselves.

Speaking declaratively from our own consciousness about what we see and know about someone else is so impactful and healing. When someone is in the midst of a challenge, they are often incapable of knowing the truth for themselves. A prayer spoken as "we" can trigger a rejection of Truth. It can be a reminder, "They may be saying I am strong and capable, but I really don't know that I am strong, I've never been strong, I'll never be strong," and they are back in their story, negating the power of affirmative prayer to realign their understanding.

Condition and Purpose

When we are praying with others, the purpose of the prayer flow emerges in the same way as our personal prayer flow. We listen to what has brought this person to prayer, and we discern what spiritual principle would be useful right now. Once again, we are not deciding for them and telling them what we think they need. We are listening for what would be useful. Often the divine principle is fairly obvious.

I just want to feel real connection and love with my sister.

I am so anxious about this. I want to be at peace with everything.

I am so tired of doubting myself. I want to have faith in me.

They have identified the purpose and articulated it for themselves. In the examples above, the divine principles most useful now would be love, peace, and faith. Even if what they request would not have been what we would have chosen for ourselves, we do not insert our desires into their prayer request. We honor their inner wisdom and focus the prayer around what would be useful to them.

Sometimes what would be useful is not as obvious as the above examples. Sometimes there is so much going on in their prayer request that you may have heard five or six different possibilities. In those moments you can directly ask those you are praying with, "What would you like anchored in this prayer?" This question releases you from deciding for them. It invites them to gain clarity as to what they believe would shift their consciousness. You can ask them directly as the conversation illustrates in the example below:

What would you like anchored in this prayer?
I am so lost and confused, I don't know what I need.
Perhaps wisdom would support you to gain clarity?
Wisdom maybe, but I really just want to feel grounded and centered.
So is it strength in the midst of all that is happening right now?
Yes! Strength, to know my inner strength.

Just as with our personal prayer practice, the more we practice listening and praying with others, the more mastery we will develop. The challenges that arise as we pray with others are linked to what we understand about our role as a prayer partner. Let's look at some of the most common stumbling blocks we can encounter when praying with others.

Common Misunderstandings When Praying with Others

Praying with others may seem to you to be a most natural act, stemming from genuine care for the spiritual well-being of others. It may feel like a calling, as gentle as a heart tug or an urgent intuition. Whether you decide to pray with others as another step on your spiritual path or by the urging of those who regard you as a supportive presence, whether you feel eager or hesitant to fulfill such a purpose, praying with others can be a rewarding act of service. It can also seem daunting.

Any form of prayer, especially affirmative prayer as taught in New Thought, presents some challenges we want to address to clarify the role of one who prays with others. When you are the person praying with others—whether you are in the role of minister, practitioner, chaplain, or even a supportive friend—the challenges are yours, not theirs.

Meeting Them Where They Are

A common concern of prayer leaders is meeting those we pray with *where they are*. The concern is usually voiced by someone studying affirmative prayer when they think of praying with someone unfamiliar with New Thought. It is understandable, and thoughtful, to conceive of meeting others where they are. Unfortunately, it often means shortchanging the person by reciting rote prayer or reverting to embedded theology you no longer support.

By all means, begin where they are. Listen, reflect on what they have said, even start by employing vocabulary familiar to theirs based upon their religious affiliation—just do not leave them there! Remember that they asked for prayer support and you have cultivated a consciousness of prayer for that purpose. Remember the purpose of affirmative prayer is a shift in consciousness leading to empowerment. We reiterate this guideline from the cofounder of Unity prayer, Myrtle Fillmore:

> Our spiritual ministry is only half done unless we give those unto whom we minister an explanation of the Christ principles that will enable them to demonstrate spiritual laws for themselves.
> —Letter in the Myrtle Fillmore Collection

Falling Into Their Story

A good story can captivate our attention. The details can surprise or disturb us. When someone shares their story with us before we pray with them, we can get lost in the story. We can begin to imagine ourselves in the story. Or we can be triggered to recall a similar story from our own experience. Or we might begin to confuse the conditions of the story with the truth. To avoid falling into their story, we need to know the boundary between them and us. We also need to know the boundary between their story and their identity, their story and their spiritual capacity. The greatest gift in prayer support is that we see with spiritual eyes the truth of their divine identity.

To listen with empathy rather than sympathy is key to being a helpful prayer partner. As we define the words, *sympathy* is sharing in someone's feeling, in a sense blurring the boundary between them and us. *Empathy* is understanding without bearing the feelings of others.

Whether a person asking for prayer tells a lengthy story with a plethora of details and tangents or presents a laundry list of prayer requests that includes many people and their conditions, you as the leader of the prayer need to recognize when it is time to move from the request into prayer. Pay attention for an opening or gently interrupt the speaker. If you are unclear about what is most pressing for the person, you can say something to the effect of, "We will hold all your concerns in prayer, those you have mentioned and those not spoken, and we want to pray specifically about what seems most essential to you in this moment." Then, in prayer, remind them of their true nature and capacity to shift their thoughts and actions going forward.

Trusting Spirit to Put the Words in Your Mouth

We are absolutely in favor of inspired prayer. We believe that when we are prepared through study and training, and steeped in spiritual practice, our words of prayer will reflect it. However, we hear of students who, with very little study or training, have been told to "just go to your heart" and whatever comes out of your mouth will be perfect.

Our experience is that what comes out of our mouths when we pray is what we have practiced. What we know in our bones, what we were taught and have believed, what is familiar—all that flows when we let it flow.

To lead affirmative prayer and to facilitate spiritual transformation, you must study spiritual principles and engage in spiritual practice. There is no shortcut and no substitute for building prayer consciousness.

Praying for Their Requested Outcome

Another trigger for those who pray with others is feeling lured into praying toward a stated outcome. We want as much as they do for their loved one to get well, their job interview to land them that job, or their lost pet to be found. But this is not why we pray or what we pray about.

In a 1927 booklet published by Unity and mailed to first-time prayer callers, the Unity prayer ministry instructed:

> We do not pray for people to receive the multitude of "things" for which they ask; neither do we pray for specific results in personal matters. For example, we do not pray that a certain person may be influenced to buy a piece of property, or that one may obtain a particular position that he may have in mind; nor do we pray that anyone may fall in love with, or become engaged to or married to

another. The real need of each one is for wisdom, understanding, and good judgment, and it is for these that we pray.

—Instructions for Those Receiving
the Ministry of the Silent Unity Society

These instructions point to the need for us to identify the spiritual issue behind a prayer request. Refer to earlier pages in this chapter where identifying the purpose or spiritual issue is discussed in detail. Here is an example of how to ensure praying effectively with someone who is asking for a specific outcome.

With the person requesting healing for their child undergoing surgery, instead of affirming that the surgery goes well, you could affirm that you are *centered in the principles of order and wisdom* and invite them to affirm that they, their child, and their medical team are centered in those principles as well. You could speak of realizing order as each adjusts to the circumstances moment by moment and realizing wisdom to make sound decisions going forward. You could choose different principles such as life, which is their power to know wholeness and well-being, or faith, their power to perceive the truth of wholeness even in moments when it seems elusive.

Of importance is a reminder that someone's stated desire is not always what they most want. Someone praying for a Maserati might want a symbol of prosperity or a reliable form of transportation for their family or a sense of thrill and adventure. Listen for a spiritual issue and support their claim of a spiritual principle.

Trying to Fix Them of It

Another paragraph from the 1927 publication mentioned earlier reads:

Many persons think that we are going to take them right up and heal them without their having to do a single thing. We do not make any such claim.

135

Our methods all lead up to the bringing forth of the health and perfection that are always ready to manifest in the one who gives them a chance.

—Instructions for Those Receiving
the Ministry of the Silent Unity Society

Thinking their healing is our responsibility or labeling ourselves "healer" is completely backward. We are not problem-solvers when we pray with others. At best, we are facilitators of spiritual transformation. Remember two essential facts:

1) The only place where prayer happens is within your consciousness. Your realization in prayer is what you speak of when you pray with another. In prayer, you lend your realized consciousness to others.

   The answer to prayer is in the prayer when it is prayed.

   —Ernest Holmes, Science of Mind

2) You do not heal. God does not heal. God is the healing power itself. The person you pray with heals as they realize their divine identity and demonstrate Truth themselves. As Jesus said in Matthew 9:22, "Your faith has made you well."

Focusing on a Third Party

The person asking for prayer is the person seeking a shift in consciousness. But often the requestor wants the focus to be on healing for their loved one. Who is requesting prayer?

When praying with others we are always first and foremost praying with the person who is right in front of us. If someone is requesting prayer for another, it's because they themselves feel concerned. We can absolutely pray for those who are not present as well, while supporting the requestor with how this condition is impacting them.

As an example, Sheena has requested a prayer of healing for her brother Ahmed who is in the hospital. You can gently inquire, "And how can I support you in prayer as well?" The opening this creates allows the person requesting prayer to feel supported as well. Your prayer can incorporate what has brought Sheena to the prayer field while also anchoring Ahmed in healing and wholeness.

Encouraging Spiritual Bypass

One of the primary teachings in New Thought, the law of mind action, is classically stated: "Thoughts held in mind produce after their kind." The teaching stresses that our feelings and the ideas, attitudes, and beliefs we harbor become major influences on how we experience life. In other words, positive attitude and outlook leads to positive experiences and vice versa.

The law of mind action, meant to steer us away from negative patterns of thinking, is so foundational in New Thought that well-meaning metaphysics students learn a kind of vigilance that reveals misunderstanding. It plays out by actions such as guarding every spoken word, as if expressing the merest worrisome thought would lead to a terrible circumstance, or disallowing negative feelings for fear they would dominate and multiply. Skipping over negative thoughts or disallowing feelings is known as spiritual bypass.

Granted, training and experience help us to navigate the both/and of the law and its consequences. We are encouraged by the current-times insistence on allowing for feelings before shifting toward Truth. It is a kinder, gentler approach and consistent with the practice of negation and affirmation by which we can recognize and release thoughts that produce negative emotions before affirming a needed truth. Notice we are not negating feelings but thoughts that produce them. For example, instead of negating that I am frustrated with how slowly my physical rehabilitation seems to be going, I would instead negate the belief that there is a specific timetable my rehab must adhere to, and if it doesn't happen on that timetable, then I am somehow not going to get better.

Prayer leaders in training sometimes express concern that the affirmative prayer flow can come across as cold or clinical rather than compassionate. They are missing the comfort of a supreme being who will take care of them, and principle therefore can seem impersonal. Yet affirmative prayer grounded in principle need not be cold or clinical. In fact, before you pray, at the moment you first interact with a person, you are able to connect human to human as well as spirit to spirit. Your compassionate heart can open to embrace them without bearing their burdens.

To avoid spiritual bypass, honor the human thoughts and feelings shared by a person requesting prayer. Never tell them their thoughts or feelings are wrong or unimportant. Acknowledging them, paraphrase the content of their sharing so they may feel reassured that you understand. Let them know their thoughts and feelings are appropriate, whatever they may be.

Honor human thoughts and feelings, yes, but do not linger in the human condition. Once acknowledged, feelings begin to calm as you move into the prayer flow. The opening of prayer provides spaciousness for the person to begin to shift into recognition, then integration, then realization, after which they are likely to experience appreciation for their shift in consciousness.

Remember that truth is not a bandage to lay over a wound but a medicine to internalize and heal. Acknowledging thoughts and feelings is acknowledging the 100 percent human. Reminding them of the truth of their divine identity is acknowledging the 100 percent divine.

Generalizing

Just as lack of specificity can be a challenge in personal prayer, it is also a common challenge when praying with others. Generalizing sounds like platitudes such as *let us know that all is well; let us remember that God is in charge; everything is just as it should be; God is with you;* or *it's all good.*

While these statements may at first appear supportive, the problem with generalizing is twofold: One, platitudes are not affirmations of Truth, and two, generalizing does not lead toward integration or realization. Generalizing goes nowhere.

Recall that an affirmation is a statement of Truth about the nature of oneness, a spiritual principle that can be recognized, integrated, and realized. Referring to "God" without recognizing a specific divine principle leaves the person hanging, with nothing to do except wait for God to act.

Furthermore, principles such as love, life, and strength encompass many and varied aspects. To facilitate a person's integration and realization, provide a descriptive adjective when recognizing principles—for example, the unifying power of love, the vitality of life, or the courage of strength. Think in terms of how a person you are praying with might move into action or realization.

An example is the harmonious power of love, identified and recognized in prayer with someone wanting to improve their relationship with a member of their family. The word *love* by itself is so broad that it can leave the person thinking vaguely, *I can be more loving.* But that is nonspecific and hard to actualize. Include the word *harmonizing*, however, and now you are alluding to the person's spiritual capacity for harmonizing their thoughts as well as speaking words specifically to cultivate harmony in the relationship.

Sharing the Gift of Affirmative Prayer

This chapter has focused on common pitfalls and challenges when praying with others. Perhaps those challenges can feel a little daunting. Know that your willingness to build your own prayer consciousness to be in service to others is a powerful calling. The more you practice affirmative prayer, the more affirmative prayer transforms you. As you grow your prayer consciousness these pitfalls and challenges fall away. A certainty and clarity of Truth arises, and it becomes easier to share this with the world. There is nothing more enlivening than bringing

our own transformation to the world by sharing the gift of affirmative prayer.

> Along with my spiritual practices of medita-
> tion, affirmative prayer, and visioning, what cata-
> lyzes my sense of aliveness is putting those prac-
> tices into action by being of service to others.
> —Michael Bernard Beckwith, Founder and
> CEO of the Agape International Spiritual Center

REFLECT AND PRACTICE

⊚ As you consider condition and purpose, write examples of how you can apply spiritual principle to any condition.

> *In the midst of_____, I recognize*
>
> *God is_____, so I*
>
> *can_____.*

⊚ Looking at the common misunderstandings, which are the most active for you in your current prayer practice? What specific study and practices will deepen your prayer consciousness?

⊚ Continue to write your prayers using the affirmative prayer flow template at the end of Chapter 7.

CHAPTER 10
Evolving Your Prayer Style and Vocabulary

Now that we have prepared the way and described the prayer flow as it applies to praying with others, we turn our attention to style and vocabulary. While we reiterate that there is no wrong way to pray, there is a distinct flow to New Thought affirmative prayer. As you gain experience in the prayer flow, it is essential for you to develop your prayer style and vocabulary.

Point of View

A common question in training for prayer leaders is, "Should I pray in first person, second person, or third person?" It is a significant question. Like you, we have heard prayer modeled in each of these points of view. Like you, we each have our preference. Let's consider the potential benefits and drawbacks of each point of view.

First Person

First person "I" is primarily used for our own personal prayer life. When we are realizing something about our self in prayer, we would say "I can, I have, I know." We are speaking from the I, from an inner awareness. When leading prayer with another person, first-person point of view is usually preceded by an instruction to the effect of, "Let my words be your own." The prayer is then spoken as personal prayer. The one who is praying is inviting the prayer petitioner to claim *I open, I recognize, I integrate, I realize*, and *I appreciate*. An example for someone whose purpose is to make better decisions:

> *Let my words be your own: I am divine wisdom, knowing my way ahead step by step.*

Offering prayer in first person can be helpful in certain circumstances. First-person prayer can be inspiring when leading a group in prayer, such as during a church service or to begin or conclude a meeting. We have found that it can be effective as a model for a student of New Thought. It can be useful for a person who appears on the verge of a breakthrough in understanding, a way to put words in their mouth.

One drawback of first-person prayer is the possibility that the person praying conducts the prayer from and for their own personal perspective. Prayer is always from our consciousness but in service to the person we are praying with. Of course, we want to unite in heart and mind with the person. We also want to be careful not to presume to know the content of their consciousness.

Careful listening will guide your discernment about when to approach prayer with others in first-person point of view.

Second Person

Speaking directly to the requester is praying in second person. Addressing them by name and using the pronouns *you* and *your*, the person praying is reminding the requester of the Truth about them, for them to realize. Continuing the example begun above, second-person voice affirms:

> *You are divine wisdom, knowing the way ahead step by step.*

Praying in second person is probably most common in one-on-one prayer within Unity. Proponents of second-person prayer are drawn to the connection "you" creates with the other person as we pray. There is a personal-ness to this voice. It is a way to demonstrate that we see them and are with them, that these words and this divine understanding are for them personally. The second person can feel comforting and loving. It can be powerful to hear someone say directly to you, *I know who you are. I know your divine identity.* The Unity Prayer Ministry has long used the second person voice in affirmative prayer.

A drawback of second-person prayer style is the potential for directing or preaching rather than praying. As the most conversational style of the three, second-person point of view requires clarity about the role of praying with others.

Third Person

Praying in third person affirms what the person praying knows is true about the requester. They speak about the requester's divine identity, speaking aloud their name and using the pronouns she/her, he/him, or they/them. An example would be:

> *Susan is divine wisdom; she knows the way ahead step by step.*

Third person supports an objective observation of Truth. The Truth we are seeing, recognizing, and realizing is the divinity that we all are. Praying in third person can be valuable for a person hearing a message about themselves that comes from an enlightened consciousness. Instead of getting caught in their human experience, they have a chance to view themselves objectively, just as the person praying has. Third person is speaking *from* the I AM, from the absolute to the absolute of them—not speaking *to* them. There is also power in using someone's name. Hearing our name spoken in connection to our divine identity rather than our personality can be transformative. Centers for Spiritual Living and Agape have long used the third-person point of view in affirmative prayer.

In some cases, someone speaking in third person might be perceived as aloof or intellectualizing, as if they are channeling and not present. Another drawback could be a perception of praying *for* rather than *with* another person.

All three points of view have strengths and are available for you to experiment with and explore. As you gain experience praying in each point of view, you will gravitate toward one that becomes your preference. Whichever your preference, pray authentically.

Practice by Writing

Affirmative prayer, with practice, becomes extemporaneous, spoken from our deepest personal expression. Speaking from the heart supports intimacy as well as transformation. Engaging in the creative process through each of the five movements builds the consciousness of the person praying. Strengthening skill and consciousness happens over time, with training and practice.

Stepping into praying with others for the first time, drawing upon all that we have been learning while aiming to be fully present in the prayer encounter, is empowering. It can also be uncomfortable, wanting to be in our heart while at the same time needing to be conscious about the flow of the prayer.

To pray with others requires building skill and experience. It takes time and repetition. Be compassionate with yourself as you practice. Here are some suggestions for moving in the direction of praying extemporaneously:

- ⊚ Study prayer principles. Training is never one and done but continual. Learn as you reread texts and hear prayer modeled by others. Long after you have mastered praying extemporaneously, continue to read written prayers and training texts to stay fresh and reliant upon an expansive body of knowledge.

- ⊚ Practice writing your prayers.

- ⊚ Write scripts for prayers based upon the most frequently requested prayer concerns. In the Unity Prayer Ministry known as Silent Unity, the most requested prayers concern healing, prosperity, inner peace, guidance or wisdom, and world peace. Write prayers for each and reread them in preparation for praying with others.

- ⊚ Study and build your knowledge of a handful of commonly referenced principles or powers, such as love, strength, peace, and life. These principles or powers can be readily applied to many different prayer concerns.

- ⊚ Build your own outline with key words and phrases to draw from as starters for each of the prayer movements. You can keep your outline with you as you pray with others, until you internalize the flow and no longer need notes.

Stand in Your Spiritual Authority

Prayer is a practice that consciously seeks to elevate and lift our understanding beyond our human experience. When we are praying with others, we are not having a conversation with them; we are speaking from spiritual authority as the I AM. We are declaring Truth. We are speaking aloud the reality of their divine nature. As we activate our divine authority we are consciously welcoming the creative power that is available to us. This asks us to shift out of a human-to-human conversation into a living demonstration of oneness. Speaking, activating, claiming from our divine spiritual authority is an embodied experience of oneness; we are expressing an elevated consciousness.

Contact and Connection

"Should my eyes be closed or open when I pray with others?" "Is it okay to hold hands or place my hands on their shoulders?" These questions from trainees point to the importance of making a meaningful connection when we pray.

Closing our eyes and inviting the person we are praying with to close their eyes is a common practice. It stems from wanting no interference from external stimuli when we pray. It can indicate that this is a sacred moment, set apart from less formal encounters. It can be powerful.

Opening our eyes when praying with someone is also sacred. Many people avoid opening their eyes while leading prayer because of the intimacy of the act of beholding another person in the fullness of their divine humanity. Or they feel nervous speaking from spiritual authority so directly. However, imagine someone praying with you, beholding your divine humanity, and speaking your name, declaring to you what they know is true about you. Powerful.

There is no right or wrong in choosing to open or close our eyes when praying with others. We advise practicing both ways to feel which is most authentic. Notice feelings, hesitation, or resistance about one way or the other. The most important choice is to be fully present, speaking from spiritual authority.

Physical contact is an act of intimacy not to be presumed. When we know the person and are certain that it would be appreciated, and it supports rather than detracts from the prayer experience, physical contact can be meaningful. However, a person asking for prayer support is in a vulnerable position. We cannot truly know what would be best for them. When you feel inclined to reach for their hands or to place your hand on their knees or to embrace them, please ask. Ask before extending your hands; otherwise, the person could interpret this as your expectation. Say something like, "Would it support you if I were to hold your hands?"

Developing an authentic style when praying with others is not to solidify it once and for all time. In fact, a person skilled at praying with others is able to adjust style choices to meet the need of the person they are praying with at the moment. Conscious practice of various options strengthens our ability to pray with anyone and everyone.

Power of the Word

New Thought teachings emphasize that thoughts and beliefs have definite effects. The thoughts we think, and therefore the words we speak, are significant. When praying, we are responsible for speaking or writing messages of Truth. Words chosen to convey prayer messages matter.

We hear, and we agree, that consciousness matters as much as the words we speak. We hear this usually from those who believe that too much emphasis is given to the words, and that the intent to support others in prayer is enough. Words do not matter as much as intent, they say. We disagree. Words matter as much as intent.

Words matter because words represent consciousness and bring about definite effects. While praying, words reveal our understanding and belief about the divine ideas or principles behind them. This is why continual study and meditation upon Truth principles is crucial when we engage in praying with others. As we cultivate spiritual understanding, our words in prayer become definite, clear, and impactful.

Our words spoken in prayer convey spiritual authority, and they have definite effects on both the speaker and the listener.

> Every time we speak we cause the atoms of the body to tremble and change their places. Not only do we cause the atoms of our own body to change their position, but we raise or lower the rate of vibration and otherwise affect the bodies of others with whom we come in contact.
> —Charles Fillmore, *Christian Healing*

The adage "Think before you speak" applies to prayer. Charles Fillmore advised that we dwell upon the meaning of divine ideas or principles.

> The ideas that make words constructive are life, love, wisdom, substance, power, strength, and all other ideas that express divine attributes. Words carrying the life idea produce a vitalizing and life-giving effect. Words that express divine love are harmonizing and unifying in their effect.

> Words are made active in the body through their being received by the mind and carried into the body through the subconsciousness by one's thought. Constructive words that renew the body are made a part of the body consciousness by prayer and meditation.
> —*Metaphysical Bible Dictionary*

The Word is the creative process in action. First we catch hold of a divine idea or principle. We dwell upon its meaning, charging the idea with thoughts and emotions that provide context. We speak the word, the idea or principle, into expression. When we pray with someone, we draw upon a principle, shape it with our words describing its creative capacity, remind the person that the principle is the Truth of their nature, and empower the person to express the principle in the circumstances surrounding their prayer request.

Speaking our prayers aloud is a powerful act of manifestation. Practice forming vocabulary that is active, specific, clear, and actionable.

Active Rather Than Passive Voice

Speaking or writing prayer in active voice means the subject is the actor. Speaking or writing in passive voice means the subject is acted upon. One of the clearest indicators of spiritual understanding shows in the claim of spiritual authority occurring in active voice. In our experience, the difficulty of accepting *I am divine* shows in the difficulty of expressing prayer in active voice.

Notice distinctions in the following examples:

> *The Spirit of divine order is at work in your life, establishing justice, peace, prosperity, and true success.*

> *You are divine order, walking successfully step by step through life's challenges and changes.*

The first statement is passive, conveying the idea that divine order is acting upon you. The second statement is active, reminding you that you embody and express divine order.

Here are some additional examples:

Justice
Passive: *You release this situation into God's care and keeping. You know that God's law of love and justice are at work, providing the best possible outcome for all concerned.*

Active: *As a divine human, understanding and wisdom are yours. Centered in the knowledge of oneness, you rely upon spiritual insight and discernment every step of the path ahead while seeking justice.*

Healing
Passive: *I release this situation to God. I let go of all past expectations of myself and others. I am healed by God's love, peace, and forgiveness. I am free to begin anew.*

Active: *Through the power of divine love, I release and let go of negative thoughts that result in negative feelings. I claim the harmonizing power of divine love. I forgive, and I am free.*

Protection
Passive: *In everything Eva does, everywhere she goes, God protects her. Eva trusts in divine wisdom and the common sense God gives her to see her safely along life's journey. God's love protects her always.*

Active: *God is Eva's source of wisdom and courage. Centered in this awareness, she claims wisdom to discern necessary steps for her safety, and Eva claims the courage to proceed. Embodying wisdom and courage, she is at peace.*

Say What You Mean

Most of us have learned a formula for praying that we have heard repeatedly, modeled by others for us. Although Unity communities are by no means homogeneous, certain phrases are common and could be considered inside jargon or Unity-speak. Some prayer patterns stem from your personal embedded theology, including duality and anthropomorphism. Others lean toward traditional Christianity, such as beginning every prayer with "Dear God," addressing a deity.

We are in favor of vocabulary that is specific, clear, and actionable. In other words, say what you mean. Avoid Unity-speak, embedded theology, duality or separation consciousness, and language that leans in the direction of a particular religion.

We advocate vocabulary that highlights the first and second principles taught in Unity: one power and our divine identity. Following the five movements, we encourage statements of empowerment. Develop a prayer flow of opening to truth, recognizing the nature of God as a specific principle or power, integrating I AM a divine human, realizing the potential for actualizing the principle or power, and experiencing appreciation.

Let's examine some common phrases in Unity prayer vernacular and restate them to say what we mean.

God is in charge.

The phrase is historic. It is meant to reassure. It is also problematic. It works well when circumstances are unfolding as desired, but it sets us up for a God that acts like a human, especially in cases where circumstances do not resolve as desired. To affirm *God is in charge* and then learn our loved one died rather than got well either leads to disappointment in God's seeming powerlessness or to resignation, believing God caused this outcome or it must be God's will. We believe affirmative prayer can offer a stronger, more empowering message than *God is in charge* by which a person can claim divine identity and realize their spiritual capacity under the circumstances.

Here is an example of an affirmative prayer (in third person) with Marta about her brother Parker who is in critical care.

Pausing to breathe, consciously and deeply, I open and Marta is invited to open to divine life, bathing her mind, body, and spirit in its encompassing presence. I know Marta can recognize the power of life, understanding that Parker is the fullness of vitality and wholeness regardless of his medical status. I affirm Marta's capacity, in the midst of this human experience, to know Parker's life exists apart from his physical condition and to remain centered in life. I appreciate and invite Marta to appreciate the gift of knowing life is infinite.

It is possible to provide a reassuring message that is also empowering by reminding those we pray with that the very power (love, life, wisdom, strength) they are seeking from God is already, eternally, within—that in fact it is possible to live life from that power, realizing that power as a source of their next thoughts, words, and actions.

Here are some statements that you could substitute for *God is in charge*. These statements are useful in the second movement of affirmative prayer, recognition.

God is the source of prosperity within you.

Divine power is present wherever you are.

Or use these as starting places for saying what you mean in the core of affirmative prayer (recognition, integration, and realization):

God is the source of prosperity within you. You

are the prospering power, which means you can give and receive generously and experience appreciation for thriving in every moment.

Divine power is present wherever Alex is. As they claim spiritual power, Alex is able to concentrate single-mindedly on their studies.

Note: You may want to ascertain the preferred pronouns of the person requesting prayer. In this case, Alex prefers *they* and *their*.

Let go and let God.

Everyone knows what it means to say *let go and let God*. That is to say, everyone has their own understanding of the phrase. They might explain, "I know it sounds like abdicating responsibility and giving it over to a deity, but I understand that it means to release my anxiety and open space for healing." Okay, say that! Here are some options:

As I let go of thoughts leading to anxiousness, I open to inner wisdom.

Releasing belief that there could be only one right solution, you allow your divine imagination to envision next possibilities.

As he gives up frightening imaginings, Marcus is able to turn his thoughts to all that could go well.

Not as concise and alliterative as *let go and let God*, we know, but more specific, clear, and actionable.

It's all in divine order.

Our experience is that this phrase is recited at times when

we cannot figure out why something unwanted has happened. It must be divine order, we say. It is another way of saying, "It must be God's will" or "If it's meant to be, it will be." As we have been sharing, though, divine order is a spiritual principle that can be claimed, realized, and actualized. Divine order is never an imposed outcome, something that happens to us. Some other ways to give a reassuring message:

As you claim the adjusting power of divine order, you can be flexible even as you proceed in the direction of your dreams.

By the power of understanding, Sam can listen to his heart and mind for insight and a sense of direction going forward.

In the midst of this sorrow, I draw from the unifying power of divine love. Embodying love, I know I am ever one with my beloved.

Here are some additional ways to say what you mean rather than recite a statement that would require explanation or interpretation.

Instead of *God is with you*:

God is the light/love/wisdom/life/strength/power that you are.

Instead of *God's will for me is*:

Divine life/peace/love is my name and nature. God and I are one.

Instead of *he trusts God*:

He can trust his inner knowing born of divine wisdom.

Instead of *God knows your need*:

God is the source of all the love/strength/wisdom you need and desire.

Instead of *God bless you*:

You are a blessing and you are blessed.

I bless you with peace of mind/a heart full of love/a grateful heart.

Affirmative prayer offers us a practice where we can bring intention and curiosity to how we understand, conceptualize, and live into oneness. As we can see from the myriad examples in this chapter, language matters. The vocabulary we use will be the basis for our own unique style, for our prayer voice. Our language reflects our consciousness. Our work is to always be exploring, expanding, and developing our consciousness, so our language will also shift. Notice where your understanding has grown but your language has not. Look for new ways to articulate what is essentially beyond words.

REFLECT AND PRACTICE

◎ As you listen and pay attention to the words you use, what do you notice? As you speak to yourself, as you speak to others, are your words aligned in Truth?

◎ What is the consciousness your words seem to be arising from? Are they actually the words/consciousness you wish to give power and authority?

◎ Jot down some of the words and phrases that you find yourself using over and over again. Do they align with your divine identity? What types of words could you use instead?

◎ Write your own replacement affirmations for these common statements:

  ◎ Let go and let God.
  ◎ God is in charge.
  ◎ God's will for you is ...
  ◎ God bless you.
  ◎ God is with you.

◎ Record yourself praying aloud. Notice your use of language. Where do you get stuck on common phrases that don't say what you mean? How can you develop your vocabulary?

CHAPTER 11
PRAYING THE FIVE MOVEMENTS WITH OTHERS

Now that we have looked at the various style and vocabulary choices that are available to us, let's take a look at applying the affirmative prayer flow to the way we pray with others, and distinguishing it from our own personal prayer practice.

When we pray with others, we begin just as we would begin for our personal prayer life. Remember, the prayer is happening in our consciousness. The prayer flow is designed to align our consciousness with oneness. When we pray with others we are building and expanding on this understanding, so we are sharing or "lending" our consciousness of oneness. It is analogous to putting our own oxygen mask on before assisting others with theirs. We align and remember our own wholeness, and then we speak from the I AM. This integrated consciousness is what gives our prayers power. This integrated consciousness is where we derive spiritual authority. This integrated consciousness is what we are sharing with others.

One of the greatest truths for those who regularly pray with others is just how much it supports our own personal growth. When we pray with others we must first align and know Truth for ourselves before we can know Truth for someone else. Whatever is brought to us in prayer is an invitation to know for ourselves what is true. That is powerfully transformative work. Often, whatever is alive in our own life as a challenge or growing edge will show up in the prayer requests of the people we are praying with. We are always starting with our own consciousness, and that means doing our own healing and realigning so we are clear enough to share with others in an impactful way. Every prayer request is an opportunity to know our divinity more fully. The prayer process when praying with others is not *for them*; it is a process that enables us to awaken more deeply to *our own divinity*, know that our divinity is their divinity, and then share that realization with others.

Let's take a look at how we move through our own awakening and invite the person we are praying with to join us.

I Open

This movement is an invitation both for ourselves and whoever asked for prayer. We are inviting them to open along with us. The very fact that they have asked for prayer demonstrates a willingness to shift to a new understanding. We don't want to tell them to open and relax—we want to include them as *we* open and relax. *I open* with others can sound like this:

> *In this moment the invitation is to open our hearts and breathe, consciously releasing any tension or story, opening into a new understanding.*
>
> *How good it is to be present with Sam right now, opening our hearts into his prayer request for*

a new understanding, a new way of being with family.

I open into infinite possibilities, and I invite Sam to let go of worry and step into his divine potential.

In this moment the invitation is to relax—releasing the story, the tension, the worries and fears— opening and allowing stillness and possibility, willing to see anew.

Remember, this first step is not for them. We are not calming them down. We are not making them receptive. We are opening and inviting them to join us. We are modeling how to open by actually *being* open. Every time we engage the affirmative prayer field we are saying *yes* to our own personal shift in consciousness.

Recognize God Is

Just as in our personal prayer process, in this movement we are recognizing what would be useful right now. Only now we consider what would be useful for the person we are praying with. We are naming what they wish to access in the moment. There is not much difference in this movement from our personal prayer practice. Our language reflects ourselves and includes the person who requested prayer.

I recognize God is present as love. The harmonizing power of the Universe is right here and right now, that which strengthens connections and unites us all.

I recognize God is present as abundance, the overflow that is everywhere present, the plenty

that is all around us and is always available and
accessible.

Integrate I AM

In the integration movement we expand from our own I AM-ness to include the I AM-ness of the person we are praying with. We do this by seeing and acknowledging their divinity. We first acknowledge oneness for ourselves, and from there, we can easily acknowledge oneness for them.

Example of integration (third person):

When I say that God is love, I am saying that love is my true nature, for I AM one with the One. It is mine and as there is only one love, it is also Sarah's and Sarah's family's nature. Divine love is natural to Sarah—it is her true nature, and love is Sarah's to express.

Example of integration (second person):

When I say that God is love, I am saying that love is my true nature, for I AM one with the One. It is mine and as there is only one love, it is also yours and your family's nature. Divine love is natural to you, it is you, and love is yours to express.

Example of integration (third person):

Knowing there is only one life, one peace, and that it is my life, I know that this is also true for Maria. Peace is her true nature and true name. Peace is available and accessible to her right here and right now.

Example of integration (second person):

Knowing there is only one life, one peace, and that it is my life, I know that this is also true for you. Peace is your true nature and true name. Peace is available and accessible to you right here and right now.

Whether in second or third person, we are first anchoring our personal awareness of oneness, and then we expand and include the person we are praying with.

Realization

In realization, we are sharing what we have realized about the person who requested prayer. We have seen their divine nature and therefore we know what is possible, what they can do and be as they live into their divine nature. We are speaking what we know to be true about them, what we know is possible.

Realization in third person:

Therefore, I know Sarah can trust the love she is. She can center as love. She can be supported by love. I see that she knows how to speak, move, and choose as that love and she is empowered to be that love within her family. She can hold the thought of harmony clearly, and she can speak from the place of inner harmony in such a way that she inspires everyone in her household to deeper connection and loving communication.

Realization in second person:

Therefore, I know that you can trust the love you are. You can center as love. You can be supported by love. I see that you know how to speak, move, and choose as that love and you are empowered to be that love within your family. You can hold the thought of harmony clearly, and you can speak from the place of inner harmony in such a way that you inspire everyone in your household to deeper connection and loving communication.

Whether we use second person or third person, notice we are not telling them what they should know. We are not assuming what they may or may not have realized about themselves. We are sharing what *we* have realized about their true nature. We are speaking from the awareness in our own consciousness, not dictating theirs.

Therefore, I know you can trust the love you are.

Therefore, I know Sarah can trust the love she is.

I see that you know how to speak, move, and choose as that love and you are empowered to be that love within your family.

I see that she knows how to speak, move, and choose as that love and she is empowered to be that love within her family.

I Appreciate

For the final movement we are appreciating the new understanding, the shift that is possible for the person we are praying with. We can also appreciate them for their courage and willingness.

Appreciation in second person:

How grateful I am for the opportunity to stand with you, to appreciate your true nature and your true name. As you stand in your I AM, all the family dynamics are made new. I give thanks for your yes and your willingness. And so it is. Amen.

Appreciation in third person:

How grateful I am for the opportunity to stand with Sarah, to appreciate her true nature and her true name. As she stands in her I AM, all the family dynamics are made new. I give thanks for her yes and her willingness. And so it is. Amen.

A Complete Prayer with Others

Let's see how a prayer would look when all the movements are brought together. We will begin with the third person.

Praying with Sarah in the Third Person

Condition: Peace in Sarah's home, where family members have been fighting with one another and with her, their mother.

Purpose: Sarah claims the harmony of divine love in family relationships, leading to peace in the home.

I Open
In this moment the invitation is to open to the love and wisdom that is God, to open our hearts to the divine idea of family, allowing space for healing thoughts and a new understanding of how to experience family.

God Is

I recognize that God is love, the power and presence of harmony. Divine love is the power that unites us all with our loved ones. It is available and accessible, harmonizing and strengthening our capacity to experience and express the love of God as family.

I AM/Sarah Is

When I say that God is love, I am saying that love is my true nature, for I AM one with the One. It is mine and as there is only one love, it is also Sarah's and Sarah's family's nature. Divine love is natural to Sarah—it is her true nature, and love is Sarah's to express.

Sarah Can/Has/Knows

Therefore, I know that Sarah can trust the love she is. She can center as love. She can be supported by love. I see that she knows how to speak, move, and choose as that love and she is empowered to be that love within her family. She can hold the thought of harmony clearly, and she can speak from the place of inner harmony in such a way that she inspires everyone in her household to deeper connection and loving communication.

I Appreciate

How grateful I am for the opportunity to stand with Sarah, to appreciate her true nature and her true name. As she stands in her I AM, all the family dynamics are made new. I give thanks for her yes and her willingness. And so it is. Amen.

Praying with Sarah in the Second Person

I Open
In this moment the invitation is to open to the love
and wisdom that is God. To open our hearts to the
divine idea of family, allowing space for healing
thoughts and a new understanding of how to
experience family.

God Is
I recognize that God is love, the power and
presence of harmony. Divine love is the power that
unites us all with our loved ones. It is available and
accessible, harmonizing and strengthening our
capacity to experience and express the love of God
as family.

I AM/You Are
When I say that God is love, I am saying that love
is my true nature, for I AM one with the One. It is
mine and as there is only one love, it is also yours,
your family's nature. Divine love is natural to you,
it is you, and love is yours to express.

You Can/Have/Know
Therefore, I know that you can trust the love you
are. You can center as love. You can be supported
by love. I see that you know how to speak, move,
and choose as that love and you are empowered to
be that love within your family. You can hold the
thought of harmony clearly, and you can speak
from the place of inner harmony in such a way that
you inspire everyone in your household to deeper
connection and loving communication.

I Appreciate
How grateful I am for the opportunity to stand
with you, to appreciate your true nature and your
true name. As you stand in your I AM, all the family
dynamics are made new. I give thanks for your yes
and your willingness. And so it is. Amen.

Here is another example.

Praying with Sam in Third Person

I Open
Devoting this moment to slowing down and
breathing together, the invitation is to open the
heart and be willing to release the story, to know
more clearly and more deeply the truth about Sam
and Michelle.

God Is
I recognize, in this moment, that God is release—
the cleansing, freeing power of divine release
that is an ever-ready resource, that allows anger
and resentment to fall away with ease and grace,
that creates an opening for forgiveness and a new
understanding.

I AM/You Are
Knowing there is only one power, I know that
release is my life, I know that release is Sam's life,
and I know release is Michelle's life. I invite Sam
to affirm with me now: I am one with and now
claim the principle of release. *As the embodiment*
of release, Sam ease-fully cleanses his thoughts
of animosity and recrimination. There is a falling

away of that which no longer serves, of that which causes pain and suffering. The capacity to release is innate and fully Sam's to activate in this relationship.

You Can/Have/Know
Sam's agreement with divine release is an empowering stance from which Sam can fully realign his thoughts about his relationship with Michelle. I see that Sam can choose and act from the truth, that he can let go of the anger, that he can release his resentment and that in this release, forgiveness is possible. Sam and Michelle are integrally, eternally one and as he releases the story, an experience of inner peace is possible. Sam has the capacity to be that peace with Michelle in both verbal and nonverbal ways. Centered in peace, he approaches each interaction as an opportunity to see beyond the story as he welcomes the healing power of forgiveness.

I Appreciate
I am so grateful, and I appreciate Sam's willingness to see Michelle and this relationship anew. I appreciate the impact of his realizing release and experiencing the blessing of this realization for his life. And so it is. Amen

Praying with Sam in the Second Person

I Open
Devoting this moment to slowing down and breathing together, the invitation is to open the heart and be willing to release the story, to know

more clearly and more deeply the truth about you and Michelle.

God Is
I recognize, in this moment, that God is release— the cleansing, freeing power of divine release that is an ever-ready resource, that allows anger and resentment to fall away with ease and grace, that creates an opening for forgiveness and a new understanding.

I AM/You Are
Knowing there is only one power, I know that release is my life, I know that release is your life, and I know release is Michelle's life. I invite you to affirm with me now: I am one with and now claim the principle of release. *As the embodiment of release, you ease-fully cleanse your thoughts of animosity and recrimination. There is a falling away of that which no longer serves, of that which causes pain and suffering. The capacity to release is innate and fully yours to activate in this relationship.*

You Can/Have/Know
Your agreement with divine release is an empowering stance from which you can fully realign your thoughts about your relationship with Michelle. I see that you can choose and act from Truth, that you can let go of anger, that you can release resentment and that in this release, forgiveness is possible. You and she are integrally, eternally one and as you release the story, an experience of inner peace is possible. You have

the capacity to be that peace with Michelle in both verbal and nonverbal ways. Centered in peace, you approach each interaction as an opportunity to see beyond the story as you welcome the healing power of forgiveness.

I Appreciate
I am so grateful, and I appreciate your willingness to see Michelle and this relationship anew. I appreciate the impact of your realizing release and experiencing the blessing of this realization for your life. And so it is. Amen

As you grow in confidence, consciousness, and capacity, you can begin to intuit when second person or third person might be more impactful. You can even combine them. Here is an example that uses both.

Condition: Yvonne needs a blood transfusion and is anxious about the procedure.

Purpose: Yvonne claims the principle of health and wholeness.

I Open
Relaxing into this moment of prayer, I invite you to breathe easily, Yvonne, to direct your attention to your open heart and mind, ready to know, more than ever before, the presence of God that is your health and wholeness.

God Is
God is the power of life, divine life. This means that God is the vitality within every cell of my body and

your body. I know that the whole of divine life is present here and now, that there is no absence of life and there is no other power that could limit or impede this whole expression of divine life. God is the source of life because God is the fullness of life.

I AM/You Are/Yvonne Is
This fullness of life is all there is. I know life is mine, and I know that because you are one with God, life is yours! Yvonne, you are visible evidence of divine life, right here and now.

You Can/Know/Have, Yvonne Can/Knows/Has
Knowing this, I realize that Yvonne is able to cooperate with divine life as it appears in her body. You, Yvonne, are capable of recognizing that all your body systems are aligned with life. Life flows through every cell, atom, form, and function of your being. I see your anxiety falling away, and I see certainty of your own wholeness, of your capacity to heal and thrive flooding every dimension of your being. I know this blood transfusion is ease and grace as Yvonne rests in this innate wholeness. There is no anxiety or worry stronger than the healing power of life.

I Appreciate
How grateful I am for Yvonne's courage and willingness to be the I AM that she truly is. I appreciate her stepping out of fear and into life. I see and know that it is done. And so it is. Amen.

Practice, Practice, Practice

Cultivating and building a powerful prayer consciousness is one of the most fulfilling journeys of discovery, one that truly can make a difference in the world.

There is both an art and a craft to affirmative prayer. The more you practice the craft—honing your vocabulary, deepening your understanding of spiritual principle, familiarizing yourself with the prayer flow itself—the more you will experience the effortless art of being the prayer itself.

The place to begin is with your own prayer life. The stronger your own personal prayer practice is, the more impactful your prayers with others will become.

The invitation is to be curious as to what more there is for you to discover. Whether you are a seasoned practitioner or someone new to affirmative prayer, there is always more to discover. Through your willingness to question, reexamine, revisit, and requalify what you thought you understood, you will unlock the limitless potential that is you. And the world is waiting.

REFLECT AND PRACTICE

- Write an affirmative prayer in each of the three points of view.

- Which feels most comfortable to you? What could be the value of using the other points of view when warranted?

- Use the affirmative prayer flow template in your personal prayer practice to strengthen skill for when you pray with others.

- Here are some conditions for which people commonly seek prayer support. Choose a spiritual principle/power that could be an antidote for each of these conditions. Select two and write an affirmative prayer, following the prayer flow template, for another person.

  - Inner peace
  - Healing
  - Prosperity
  - Wisdom/guidance
  - World peace

- Compare your prayers for others with your personal prayer from Chapter 7. How do you feel you are evolving in your understanding and skill?

- Select a prayer partner with whom to exchange prayer support following the affirmative prayer flow. Follow these guidelines:

  - Select the frequency and schedule the same day and time into the future.

  - Limit the duration (10-15 minutes) and limit the content of the call to prayer.

  - Take turns sharing your prayer request/intention and praying with one another.

  - If you want to have a conversation, schedule a time precisely for interpersonal connection.

- You can also create a prayer circle. Here are some guidelines to support your purpose:

  - Decide whether your circle will be exclusive to a select group or open for anyone to drop in.

  - Create a set of agreements with confidentiality first and foremost.

  - Select frequency and schedule the same day and time into the future.

  - Determine whether the group will pray with a singular intention, such as world peace, or consider each person's prayer requests.

◉   There are many ways for the group to pray together:

◉   One leader that prays aloud.

◉   Rotate prayer leaders.

◉   Sharing the prayer, one person beginning and passing to others until everyone has contributed.

◉   Chamber of prayer, with everyone praying aloud at the same time.

Our Blessing to You

Our message to you as you cultivate prayer consciousness and pray with others is to know without question your rightful claim of divine identity. You are the light of the world as you uplift and empower everyone with whom you pray.

We envision you inspired with words that affirm a living truth that empowers each person. We envision you in spiritual realization of I AM for yourself, your loved ones, and all those you serve.

Recognizing someone is whole even when they don't know it, recognizing someone as love when they feel selfish and small, recognizing someone as abundant when they feel lacking in any area of their life, are ways you can show up as love and compassion in action.

We know what you are! You are the harmony of divine love. You are the adjusting power of divine order. You are the vitality of divine life. You are the unifying power of divine love. You are the light of the world.

—Rev. Linda Martella-Whitsett

—Rev. DeeAnn Weir Morency

Acknowledgments

Linda Martella-Whitsett
Writings of thought leaders whose teachings have inspired me, particularly Eric Butterworth, Myrtle Fillmore, Charles Fillmore, Emma Curtis Hopkins, and Neville Goddard.

Colleagues and friends, too numerous to name, in whose company I have been privileged to listen and learn.

DeeAnn Weir Morency
There are so many who have contributed and made this book possible. Thank you to Agape International Spiritual Center in California and the Centers for Spiritual Living families of ministers, teachers, practitioners, prayer partners, and fellow travelers—particularly the Agape practitioner class of 2008 and those in my Agape Sacred Circle, who have walked this journey with me for 15 years.

A deep bow of gratitude to The Big Deep, Class of 2010, at One Spirit Interfaith Seminary in New York and the spiritual community at Center for Spiritual Living Princeton, New Jersey, where my journey first began to make affirmative prayer truly accessible.

And to all the Unity prayer chaplains and Truth seekers drawn to a life of prayer whom I have touched and been touched by over the years—teachers, colleagues, and, most important, students. Thank you for your *yes*, for being willing to explore, question, and wrestle with what it truly means to stand in your spiritual authority and divine nature. Thank you for walking with me on this journey.

About the Authors

Award-winning New Thought author and Unity minister **Linda Martella-Whitsett** teaches that we are here to be the light of the world. Her message promotes humanity's innate capacities to respond to life's circumstances in spiritual maturity. After 20 years ministering in Unity communities, Linda joined the executive team of Unity World Headquarters at Unity Village, Missouri, in 2017 leading its 24/7 global prayer ministry, Silent Unity. She is also author of *How to Pray Without Talking to God: Moment by Moment, Choice by Choice, Divine Audacity: Dare to Be the Light of the World,* and *This Life Is Yours: Discover Your Power, Claim Your Wholeness, and Heal Your Life,* coauthored with her daughter Alicia Whitsett.

DeeAnn Weir Morency is an Agape practitioner, interfaith minister, and Unity minister. She has served in spiritual leadership within Unity since 2011 and is currently senior minister at Unity In Marin, California. An impactful speaker and skilled facilitator of New Thought and universal spiritual principles, DeeAnn is committed to joyfully illuminating the I AM that we all are through concrete tools and practices that support an awakened and empowered life.

B0217